D1600496

The European Communities

THE SOCIAL POLICY OF THE FIRST PHASE

Volume 1 The European Coal and Steel Community 1951–70

The European Communities

THE SOCIAL POLICY OF THE FIRST PHASE

Volume 1   The European Coal and Steel Community 1951–70

Doreen Collins

Senior Lecturer in the Department of Social Policy and Administration, University of Leeds

MARTIN ROBERTSON

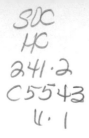
© Doreen Collins 1975

First published in 1975 by Martin Robertson & Co. Ltd., 17 Quick Street, London N1 8HL

ISBN 0 85520 083 9

B+T

Set by Trade Linotype Ltd. Birmingham
Reproduced, printed by photolithography and bound at
The Pitman Press, Bath.

Contents

Tables

Acknowledgements

I should like to thank Miss Williams of the European Communities' Information Centre, London for her help in the early stages of preparation and the staff of the Bodleian Library, Oxford for their general assistance. My colleagues, Dr and Mrs Fry and Dr Hartley gave me constructive help during some wearisome moments and for this I am most grateful. None of those mentioned can, of course, be held responsible for the contents of this volume.

I also wish to thank the University of Leeds for its generous grant towards the cost of this publication.

Abbreviations

DGB	Deutscher Gewerkschaftsbund
ECSC	European Coal and Steel Community
ECE	Economic Commission for Europe
EEC	European Economic Community
EIB	European Investment Bank
Euratom	European Atomic Energy Community
ICFTU	International Confederation of Free Trade Unions
IFCTU	International Federation of Christian Trade Unions
ILO	International Labour Organization
m.u.a.	million units of account
NATO	North Atlantic Treaty Organization
OECD	Organization for Economic Co-operation and Development
OEEC	Organization for European Economic Co-operation
u.a.	units of account
UNESCO	United Nations Educational Scientific and Cultural Organization

1 Social Responsibility under the Treaty of Paris

I Introduction

It is perhaps inevitable that the work of the European Coal and Steel Community (ECSC) should be overshadowed in the public mind by that of the European Economic Community (EEC) which would appear to embrace its functions. A study which is devoted to the ECSC is bound to some extent to appear, and indeed to be, a curtain-raiser. However, in the field of social policy there are considerable difficulties in dealing with both organizations simultaneously. In the first place, the limitation of the ECSC to a partial sector of the economy obviously gives its social responsibilities a defined range and their discussion is only meaningful within the framework of a particular industrial setting. This is not so in the case of the EEC. Secondly, the Treaty of Paris which created the ECSC gave greater powers of action to its executive, and the enlarged freedom which comes from an independent income, than was achieved by the Treaty of Rome in the case of the EEC. In consequence it would be wrong to allow the current interest in the work of the EEC to overshadow that undertaken by the ECSC which, within its limited field of competence, was nevertheless able to accomplish more. It is therefore more revealing of the potentialities of an international organization to make a contribution to the field of social policy. Finally, the work of the ECSC set a precedent which influenced the work of the later European Community. For such reasons it has been decided that it will be clearer for the reader if the powers and activities of the two organizations are kept distinct. It is to be hoped that each volume can profitably be read separately, but the close inter-relationship of the two organizations in practice and the similarity of their work mean that the more general discussion of the social functions of the European organizations at the end of Volume 2 draws on the work of the ECSC as necessary.

Apart from some very brief introductory remarks the volumes are not concerned with the movement for European unity nor with the full details of the structure of the organizations themselves. These matters have been dealt with elsewhere.[1] The volumes concentrate upon work which has often been treated rather superficially by writers

1

interested in political developments in Europe. This has reflected the fact that social responsibilities have not been at the centre of the impulse to create new organizational forms. Since, however, it is now a common assumption that national governments bear a wide range of responsibility for social well-being, and since the term 'social policy' is often heard in discussions concerning the functions of the European Communities and, indeed, is the title of one of the sections of the Rome Treaty, it has seemed worthwhile to consider a number of questions pertinent to the promotion of human well-being in the context of the work of the Communities.

In the first instance, it is necessary to be clear about the nature of social policy in the European system. To a degree statements on this matter must be speculative, since much concerning the actual negotiations of the treaties remains unknown. I hope to make clear, however, that the term has a rather specialized meaning. Perhaps partly in consequence of this conception, social policy constitutes a feature of the European arrangements which has been both ambiguous in intent and weak in executive powers. Secondly, and this constitutes the major body of the works, I have attempted to examine the operation of those clauses of the treaties which go to make up the European social policy system until the end of 1970 in the case of the ECSC and 1972 for the EEC itself. It will be seen that much valuable, and often unpublicized, work has been done to execute these functions. Finally, I discuss the way in which development came to be thought of as inadequate by the European Parliament and Commission, which were anxious to see steady progress towards a united Europe and which feared lest social responsibilities would be ignored in the pursuit of economic ends. This general discussion relates to the two Communities jointly and it is natural that criticisms should have been directed more to the EEC, or to the European organizations as a total system, than to the ECSC alone, so that the dissatisfactions voiced in Parliament were increasingly concerned with the inability of the EEC to undertake decisive policies in the social field. It has, therefore, seemed more appropriate to postpone this discussion until Volume 2.

The study is not entirely a pessimistic one, however, for in recent years member states have given signs of a greater willingness to see the Communities move into a position in which they might become more involved in the pursuit of the broad goals of social progress. This is a reflection of the obvious fact that the Communities now operate in an environment very different from that perceived in 1950 when the European Coal and Steel Community was created. At the present time of writing much discussion is taking place on questions of a broadly social nature, such as the treatment of migrant workers or the extent to which collective bargaining procedures must develop on an international level. Neither question was at the centre of the negotiations which originated the

European Communities. Whilst the urge to modify institutions to provide more effective means of dealing with new problems is a hopeful sign, it is my belief that, in relation to social questions, the structure of the European organizations is deficient and cannot be adequately adapted through a process of natural evolution. Reform requires conscious decision by members. The most fundamental is their acceptance of a much stronger commitment to redistributive expenditure through the European system.

The starting-point for a discussion of the Communities as a social policy system must, however, be the actual treaties which form the foundations upon which this system has been created. Looking back on the immediate post-war world from the vantage point of 1974 one cannot but be struck by the vast changes which have occurred. The modern Europe of affluence and close international co-operation bears little resemblance to the continent of political and economic disarray to which it had been reduced by the Second World War. Yet the experience of the physical destruction and moral division which Europe had brought upon itself proved the stimulus towards the creation of new forms of political organization which it was hoped would provide a more adequate setting for economic development and for the maintenance of a political order than the nation state had hitherto achieved.

Although schemes to unite Europe are of very considerable antiquity, a convenient and common starting-point for modern endeavour is the draft declaration which the European Resistance Movements produced in July 1944 symbolizing the need felt by the representatives of many nations, including those from both sides of the conflict, to move as quickly as possible into a stage of reconciliation. This document followed a long-standing argument which links the creation of a peaceful world with the pursuit of social progress within the national community by calling for social justice and the utilization of economic wealth for the general good as well as for a federal organization of Europe. From early post-war days a fundamental debate emerged concerning the nature of European political organization and the means whereby it might be achieved, ranging from those who wished to create a fully mature federal structure immediately to those who preferred to develop closer links through traditional measures of inter-governmental action. Meanwhile the economic problems of European recovery and the rapid political changes on the continent demanded practical action. The offer of Marshall Aid led to the creation of the Organization for European Economic Co-operation (OEEC) in 1948 which in turn brought considerable experience in close co-operation in economic matters among the nations of Western Europe. The same year saw a mutual defence pact between France, Great Britain, Belgium, Luxembourg and the Netherlands, which was signed at Brussels as a reaction to a growing Communist threat. This was an agreement which accepted also the need for economic, social and cultural co-operation and which referred to the possibility of setting up a European Parliamentary Assembly. Continuing military pressure led to a link between the Brussels Treaty organization and the Nato alliance, but the belief in European integration was no longer confined to defence matters and the search for means of unity in other fields continued.

The high-water mark of the federalists was perhaps the Hague Congress of May 1948 upon which many hopes for greater European unity were focussed only to be doomed to disappointment. From the Congress stemmed the Council of Europe whose Council of Ministers and Consultative Assembly represented modest views of the future organization of Europe and whose 'limited functions but real powers' were insufficient to satisfy those seeking radical changes in European political organization. By 1949, therefore, it appeared that neither political nor economic nor military pressures had been adequate to compel the renunciation of national autonomy.

II The European Coal and Steel Community

The Schuman declaration of 9 May 1950[2] tackled the question of European organization from a new point of view. It by-passed existing debate by proposing an international authority which would have effective powers in a limited field of international concern, namely the production of coal and steel. This was portrayed as a first practical move towards the creation of a European federation which could thus emerge from a series of cumulative steps, each one being taken when the time was ripe. It therefore offered a constructive alternative to the more traditional federal approach of a direct attack on constitutional questions. Simultaneously, the creation of a new European structure suggested a means of finding a basis for Franco–German reconciliation and for allowing the restoration of Germany in a way which would prove acceptable to the West. The declaration had, therefore, two inter-related aims. Firstly, to bury Franco–German rivalry and, secondly, to take a primary step towards the creation of a Europe which would 'not be made all at once, or according to a single, general plan. It will be built through concrete achievements, which first create a *de facto* solidarity.'[3] The organization, argued M. Schuman, should be open to all and should aim to create a free market in coal and steel products thus allowing a fall in prices with consequent beneficial effects upon the standard of living. Plans for production and modernization would be required, including a fund for reconversion and rationalization. A transitional period for the necessary adjustments was proposed but it would not be necessary to interfere with the nature of industrial ownership. The system would be run by an international authority, independent of national governments, which would become responsible for the modernization programme, for the development of the free market and of exports and for the progressive equalization of the conditions of life of the workers in these industries.

The details of the precise intentions which underlay the Schuman declaration and of the negotiations which followed it and culminated in the Treaty of Paris are not publicly known.[4] It is common knowledge, however, that the declaration was based upon a draft drawn up by M. Jean Monnet with whom Paul Reuter, Pierre Uri and Jacques Gascuel were closely associated.[5] The Monnet memorandum stressed the importance of working towards a united Europe and, on the economic side, the advantages of a larger market and the rising standards of living made possible by increased production. At the same time, it recognized that some protection for the coal industry would be necessary for social reasons.[6] There is no doubt that M. Monnet's motives were essentially political.[7] As a staunch believer in a federal Europe, he was seeking a new move to achieve a breakthrough in the European situation and, as a realist, a method to ensure that a resurgent Germany found herself firmly attached to the West. This could not be achieved except on the basis of a *modus vivendi* for France and Germany. For this latter purpose, the French offer to pool those industries which formed the heart of the traditional war-making complex had profound psychological significance, although it has been suggested that M. Monnet himself thought that, as a purely practical task, it would have been easier to start on the process of European integration with newer industries.[8] At the same time he was acutely aware of the difficulties of the French economy. If this were simply to be opened to German industrial competition, France would react by creating a progressively protected system unless a way towards joint expansion could be found. Thus the starting-point for the specific plan to create the European Coal and Steel Community rested upon the argument that the time had come to build a dynamic Europe, to find a place for Germany in the Western community and to lead France into the modern world.

This bold plan received a mixed reception. Despite the overwhelming political advantage contained in a move designed to ameliorate the problem of the German position in Europe, it was clear that any such scheme was bound to have variable effects on national industries, on particular firms and on employment possibilities.[9] Reactions in political, industrial and union circles in Europe were by no means uniform, and the negotiations which subsequently led to the treaty, although carried through by governments which had previously accepted the validity of the pool principle, had nevertheless to find room for the accommodation of interests which were often opposed. Employers and unions in Holland

and Germany were generally in favour although, in the latter case, the overwhelming interest lay in the possibility the scheme offered to end allied control over her industry and in her restoration as a political equal. Belgian coal owners were particularly hostile to the plan in view of their high-cost mines, whereas the strong Belgian socialist unions favoured the possibility it gave of imposing higher wage and social charges as an obligation on all employers covered by it. Italian unions saw the opportunity of freer migration for the unemployed but this was exactly what worried the Deutscher Gewerkschaftsbund (DGB). German union leaders believed, however, that employment prospects for their members would broadly be improved in so far as the coal and steel industry benefited from the new system and that any commitment to the equalization of wages and social security benefits would be of advantage to them. A particular problem for them, however, was to protect their system of worker participation in management which had been developed in the German coal and steel industries.

The biggest psychological effort was called for from France. The French coal and steel industry was generally against the plan, fearing competition from lower-cost producers, the adverse effects of the trade cycle in an unprotected system and the imposition of supra-national planning of a type many employers still disliked at the national level and in which M. Monnet had been a driving force. It felt, therefore, that it would be seriously disadvantaged since it carried heavier wage and social charges than its competitors, that high-cost firms would have to close, that there would be a general weakening of French heavy industry and that French workers would be driven to work in Germany at lower wages than those previously available. In view of the attitude of French employers, a possible explanation of the insertion in the Schuman declaration itself of the aim of equalizing conditions for the workers is that it was a recognition of the likely reaction of certain elements among French employers as well as an appeal to which many workers would respond.

The nature of the new scheme had thus already been laid out on broad lines by the French. Shortly afterwards the six governments which had decided to pursue the matter further in the hope of achieving an agreed and detailed scheme announced the opening of the negotiations. These continued until the following March, the Treaty of Paris was signed in April 1951, submitted to ratification procedures and operative from 25 July 1952.

During the negotiations the French thesis on wage equalization failed to achieve acceptance in precise form. Its implication that the new international authority would require responsibility for wage levels and the right to negotiate directly with employers and workers, whilst carrying no responsibility for wage rates generally, was too advanced organizationally and considered impractical. Union fears concerning a fall in wage levels and of unemployment were largely canalized into demands for a consultative committee, for the executive to include one or more members acceptable to them and for safeguard arrangements rather than for direct controls over wages and other benefits. M. Schuman himself was at pains to stress that his plan was based upon the assumption of full employment and the maintenance of labour standards.[10]

The Treaty of Paris is a highly complex document whose features are only briefly sketched here to form a background to the social clauses. Politically it began the process of creating new institutions with the capacity to take international decisions yet which did not go too far for current national prejudices. Control of the Community was divided between four major institutions designed to represent various interests and different approaches to international co-operation. The key position was held by the High Authority which possessed decision-taking and executive powers but under a system of controls operated by the Council of Ministers, the Court of Justice and the Assembly. Under Art. 8 the High Authority became responsible for ensuring the achievement of the purposes of the treaty and thus for the abolition of conditions which might impede the creation of the common market (Art. 4) as well as for positive action to fulfil the wide-ranging objectives of the new system. Although on 1 July 1967 [11] the High Authority was merged with the executives of the general common market and of the European Atomic Energy Community (Euratom) to form a single Commission, the substance of its responsibilities remained the same. Certain minor flexibilities of procedure were abandoned but the main fear of the High Authority was of a loss of momentum in the social field as it became integrated into a larger body with lesser powers of initiative.[12]

The High Authority received the power to work on the basis of majority voting and to take decisions binding either on the addresses or on publication as appropriate, to formulate recommendations binding in their objectives but not their means and to issue non-binding opinions. Each form of pronouncement had to include the reasons which lay behind it and some indication of the advice received by the High Authority in so far as it was obliged by the treaty to obtain such advice (Arts. 14, 15). It was made responsible for the publication of an annual report and had power to control its own internal organization and to set up study groups (Arts. 16, 17). The High Authority itself consisted of nine people, not more than two from any member state, owing a supranational allegiance to the Community itself. The members had, nevertheless, to be acceptable to governments and during the discussion on the drafting of the treaty it was agreed that at least one member would enjoy the confidence of the trade unions. The appointments of Paul Finet (ex-President of the International Confederation of Free Trade Unions

[ICFTU]) and of the German, Heinz Potthoff, a known labour sympa-
thizer, fulfilled this commitment. They remained members from 1952 to
1965 and 1962 respectively.

The special Council of Ministers was created to represent the official
views of states, its members being drawn from governments and the
Presidency held in rotation for three-monthly periods. Membership was
not static for states sent the most appropriate minister to meetings
according to the topic before the Council. In practice this was often the
Minister for Economics. Finance or Social Affairs. The particular
responsibility of the Council was to harmonize the action of the High
Authority with that of governments as the entities responsible for the
general economic policy of their countries (Art. 26). Provision was thus
made for joint consultation and the exchange of information whilst the
Council was entitled to ask the High Authority to examine any proposals
it considered would be beneficial to the Community. An example of the
consultation procedure is to be found in Art. 68 under which the High
Authority had to consult before issuing a recommendation, to either
governments or firms, on the need to improve wage levels.

Additionally, there were occasions upon which the High Authority
needed the approval of the Council before it could move. Thus control
of the Council over the High Authority was essentially exercised by the
giving, or the refusal, of its agreement in those cases where it was
required. An example related to the right of the High Authority to raise
monies through levies on coal and steel production. Under Art. 50 (2)
this levy could not exceed 1 per cent of the annual productive value
without the Council's authorization on a two-thirds majority vote, whilst
the High Authority was bound to consult the Council before determining
the methods of assessment and collection of the levy. The Council had to
approve if production quotas were to be applied because of over-supply
or if certain restrictions on exports or imports were found to be
necessary.

In reaching its conclusions, the Council had different methods open to
it. It was unnecessary for the Council to take a vote where the treaty
obliged the High Authority to consult; it might simply record its delibera-
tions. In other cases agreement was by unanimity or by different forms
of majority voting which had to include the assent of one of the major
producers.[13] Thus, in the social field, the High Authority needed the
concurrence of an absolute majority of the Council for assistance to be
given to the development of projects outside the coal and steel industries
under Art. 56; it required the Council's unanimous approval under Art.
54 for its financial aid to housing projects but its right to call for information relevant to its responsibility to raise standards for living and working
conditions was independent of the Council.

The Paris Treaty created a Court of Justice which later became common to the three European Communities. Its essential function was to ensure the correct application of the treaty through hearing appeals against the High Authority on the basis of law. It was not the function of the Court to involve itself in the economic policies of the High Authority at the behest of those who disliked them, but to consider if the decisions and recommendations were contrary to the treaty provisions. Objections could be raised by the Council and by member states on general grounds whilst firms and their associations could appeal against both general decisions and recommendations which affected them and those which were directed towards them individually. If the Court decided against the High Authority then it had to replace the offending direction and, in appropriate cases, make redress. These same parties could also appeal to the Court if the High Authority had not taken action which it should have done under the treaty and a state could complain if it believed action of the High Authority had provoked 'fundamental and persistent disturbances in its economy' (Arts. 35, 37). The Court was also entitled to annul resolutions of the Assembly and the Council under certain circumstances.

Art. 20 created an Assembly to be composed either of delegates appointed by national Parliaments or of 'persons elected by direct universal suffrage' (Art. 21). This, too, came to serve the three Communities. It had to meet annually but the Council, the High Authority or a majority of the Assembly itself could call an extraordinary session. Apart from its dramatic right to compel the complete resignation of the High Authority on a motion of censure of the annual report carried by a two-thirds majority, the Assembly had no key place in the constitutional proceedings. In 1962 it adopted the name Parliament and this term is now generally used. It was clearly a weak feature of the Community although it did a good deal of painstaking work in relation to the study of social affairs and was normally supportive of the High Authority's attempts to develop social policy.

Additionally, the latter drew some strength from the support of the consultative committee. Although the ECSC was originally much criticized as Europe of the cartels, it did attempt to ensure that organized employer and labour organizations were brought into contact with it. Since much of the work of the High Authority to advance living and working conditions could only be educational and promotional, in which action taken at the national level was the more important, it was essential for it to have continuing contact with employers, unions and parliamentarians. The consultative committee consisted of equal numbers of producers, workers, consumers and dealers up to a total of fifty-one and was constituted on 1 January 1952.[14] Whilst it had to be consulted by the High Authority whenever the treaty so stated, it might be approached by the executive at any time and in practice it was so consulted in most cases before the High Authority took an important decision.[15] Thus the High Authority had to submit to the committee its general objectives and planning programmes before they were published (Art. 46) and keep it generally informed of its loan programme for investment purposes and of any action it took to prevent agreements inhibiting competition or undesirable concentrations of industry (Art. 19). The High Authority was bound to consult the committee before establishing production quotas to deal with a crisis situation (Art. 58) or before steps in response to actions of member states which would affect competitive conditions (Art. 67) or before sending recommendations to enterprises or governments concerning abnormally low wages (Art. 68) or if technical changes caused serious unemployment in the coal and steel industries (Art. 56).

Whilst the treaty envisaged a close, and constant, relationship between the High Authority and the committee is it equally clear that the latter existed only in an advisory capacity. Its importance depended upon the extent to which the High Authority was willing to be influenced by what the committee had to say. Since it could meet on its own initiative at the request of a majority of its members, it could ensure a steady flow of opinion and comment upon which the High Authority could call if it wished. Technically, the executive did not need to take notice of the opinions of the committee even when bound to ask for them but, in fact, in the field of social policy, the two bodies tended to find themselves in broad agreement and it was therefore to the advantage of the High Authority to discuss matters with the committee and receive its views.[16] Although the committee passed formal resolutions on the matters referred to it, the weight of opinion expressed in the reports rather than the number of favourable votes carried the more influence.[17] The tenor of the committee's opinions, particularly in social matters, was in favour of more positive action and it strongly advocated the need for the Community to develop a coherent energy policy, for the merger treaty to have a definite commitment to a full employment policy and that the creative attributes of the High Authority, such as in the field of workers' housing, should not be dropped in the merger.[18] This role was probably helped by the fact that the union representatives on the committee acted as a coherent group whereas the others were more divided.[19]

The consultative committee was not, however, the only channel of communication between the High Authority and interested parties. Art. 46 was of particular importance here because of the wide range of subjects upon which consultation and discussion might take place, and it was difficult to see how the obligations of the High Authority could be otherwise fulfilled. 'The High Authority may at any time consult the governments, the various interested parties (concerned undertakings, workers, consumers and dealers) and their associations as well as any experts' and similarly these groupings had the right to present any suggestions or observations to the High Authority on questions which concerned them. These consultations were intended partly for the purpose of enabling the High Authority to carry on a permanent study of markets and prices, to draw up non-compulsory forecasts and to develop general programmes for modernization and expansion. It was also arranged that, at the request of interested governments, the High Authority might participate in the study of the possibilities of re-employment, either in existing industries or through the creation of new activities, for workers unemployed as a consequence of the evolution of the market or technical change. The High Authority was given the right to gather all information necessary for it to fulfil its responsibility to help to improve the living and working conditions of the labour force in the coal and steel industries and to offset the risks which menaced these standards and to publish the studies made. Art. 48, paragraph 3, gave another glimpse of the importance attached to economic democracy in that it enabled the High Authority to expect producers' associations themselves to have some internal mechanism for the expression of the voices of the workers and consumers so that the information submitted to the High Authority took account of such views. Under Art. 55 the High Authority had the right to aid research and distribute its findings, and under Art. 16 to set up study groups. In such ways a wide pattern of consultation and discussion prior to the taking of decisions developed.[20]

The High Authority also encouraged contacts outside the Community where these appeared to be useful in developing understanding of current needs of the policies it wished to adopt. An early example was the Trade Union delegation sent to the United States in 1954 to study problems of retraining and re-employment of the labour force in coal and steel,[21] and a later one the management group sent to visit training schemes in Great Britain and the Community.[22] It also actively developed its own relations with labour organizations in pursuit of its belief in the importance of union support for the European movement and in labour participation in the formulation of social policy. The Dortmund Conference of 1964 at which the High Authority expounded at length its views on the need for a European miners' code, and the Menton Conference of 1966 to review the social policies of the High Authority, are good examples of this policy. Such mechanisms added up to a formidable capacity to work with non-governmental groups and to establish a close understanding between the High Authority, unions, employers, political parties, civil servants and representatives of organizations affected by the establishment of the ECSC, and a complex pattern of consultation prior to the taking of decisions developed accordingly.

The strong powers given to the High Authority and its relationship to the other institutions, notably the Council, form a major interest in the workings of the Community, for it is here that its claim to originality in the field of international organization is to be found. Whilst far-reaching powers were transferred to an international institution, their exercise was qualified by the procedures laid down in the treaty which attempted to give due regard to national interests, to the views and requirements of the coal and steel industries and of the community at large. The Community was not intended to be either international co-operation in the traditional sense or federalism but a unique structure somewhere in between and in which different degrees of supra-nationality were allowed. It was to be the *'nouvel échelon dans la gradation des pouvoirs, situé à égale distance entre l'individualisme national et la fédéralisme d'Etats'.*[23]

Different degrees of supra-nationality were allowed for in the treaty. The High Authority's responsibility to take decisions which might be operative directly on individuals and firms could, in certain fields, be exercised with no reference to any other Community institution. It thus had the right to impose its own rate of levy up to the maximum, to borrow, to grant loans, to grant certain forms of redundancy aid and to rule on the acceptability of agreements between firms. In other cases it was required to obtain the agreement of the Council and, on occasion, to have consulted the consultative committee before coming to a decision. 'The Council was conceived as a check on the powers of the High Authority in fields where the member governments were not prepared for a complete surrender of their right to influence decisions'.[24]

Not only was the High Authority given powers of independent decision, on the basis of majority vote, but it received the right to enforce its will through sanctions on defaulting enterprises, as in the case of a refusal to divulge information or to persist in projects or activities of which the High Authority disapproved. Furthermore, if the High Authority believed that a state had failed to fulfil one of its obligations under the treaty, it was obliged to approach the member with the aim of resolving the issue subject to the right of the state to appeal to the Court of Justice. Nevertheless, in practice, the powers of the High Authority were heavily circumscribed. History was to show the continuing importance of national decisions within the Community system and this, combined with the checks devised through Parliament and the Court, constituted considerable control over the supra-national process.

From the point of view of the European economy the ECSC also represented a new approach. Attempts under OEEC had concentrated upon achieving trade liberalization by the removal of quotas, and post-war recovery had been considered largely within the context of national frontiers. The Schuman plan, however, adopted the more radical procedure of starting from the premise of a free market providing the necessary safeguards for weaker competitors through the gradual introduction of the system, by making finance available for the modernization and adaptation of plant and for the resettlement and retraining of labour so that more efficient productive mechanisms might develop within the larger whole. The economic arrangements of the Treaty of Paris have often been described as stemming from neo-liberalism.[25] The text itself contained no statement of doctrine but was based rather upon the assumption of an internationally competitive system for whose creation and maintenance a set of rules was required and which it was the purpose of the treaty to provide. This did not, however, imply any particular form of industrial ownership, as was specifically stated in Art. 83, and the arrangements were sufficiently tolerant to include both nationally and privately owned industries. The creation of the conditions of effective competition was, however, only one part of the treaty system. Its further purposes were to lay down the overall objects to which the several industries should conform. Thus the arrangements under the treaty for ensuring a competitive market and competitive prices were balanced with modernizing and developmental provisions as part of the same overall scheme. The first priority was for the establishment of a common market in which there would be no possibility of independent action to impose import or export duties or quantitative restrictions on coal and steel movements, no discriminatory practices, no state assistance to the coal and steel industries and no restrictive practices dividing the market or exploiting the consumer. Thus, within the common market an effective competitive system based on open prices would operate, and states bound themselves not to take action affecting competitive conditions without notice although emergency arrangements were permitted to enable states to deal with their general economic difficulties (Art. 67). Emergency and reserve powers were placed in the hands of the Community institutions should a decline in demand lead to a crisis situation in the industries of the Community (Art. 58).

Nevertheless the Treaty of Paris did not create an unbridled competitive system but substituted positive economic objectives for the restrictive arrangements which had hitherto existed as the framework within which the industries should operate. With the signature of the treaty, the Community became responsible for contributing to economic expansion, to the development of employment and the improvement of the standard of living in participating countries, for establishing conditions suitable for the rational distribution of production, high productivity, safeguarding the continuity of employment and avoiding serious disturbances in the economies of the members (Art. 2). It was thus a system of controlled competition in which the general community welfare would be served by the larger market and the greater efficiency of production this would bring, the individual producer would be helped if necessary to adjust to the new circumstances and the interests of the worker in the coal and steel industries would be safeguarded in various ways.

The Community was not made directly responsible for the operation of the coal and steel industries but for the establishment of a framework within which they might operate, supported by the agreement of the members not to take measures incompatible with the existence of the common market. Future development would be influenced by the Community through the obligation placed on the High Authority to produce general objectives setting out forward-looking plans for the whole of the area (Art. 46) and its rights to insist upon receiving information concerning individual development projects and to express an opinion on them. Where such a plan required aid from outside the firm the High Authority was able to forbid it (Art. 54) and through its ability to aid investment it had a positive tool with which to influence development. Investment programmes were to be eligible for financial aid either in the form of low-interest loans or as guarantees so that firms might gain access to capital markets.[26] Financial aid was additionally made available for capital expenditure by firms, whether within Community industries or not, for the purpose of re-employing redundant workers from coal and steel and for the retraining and support of workers themselves (Art. 56). A decision aimed to increase production, reduce costs or facilitate marketing required unanimous support from the Council, job creation to absorb the redundant into industries other than coal and steel required a concurring opinion from the Council,[27] whilst aid in the creation of jobs within the coal and steel industries themselves lay within the discretion of the High Authority. By these provisions the Community was put in a position to play an active part in economic development through influencing the fortunes of individual firms and of the regions of heavy industry. At the same time no clear indication was given in the treaty of the role to be played by economic planning either on the national or the international level. The system was wide enough to incorporate both indicative planning and the heavily liberal approach of the German governments of the 1950s, whilst the provisions for the High Authority to establish general objectives were too weak to be considered as they stood as serious Community planning. In this, as in many ways, the Community economic system was incoherent, leaving room for adaptation and evolution under changing economic and political influences.

A transitional period of five years from the date of setting up the common market in coal was created by an annexed convention which allowed for the continuance of protective devices in certain defined circumstances and imposed a temporary equalization levy on low-cost producers for the benefit of those with above average costs. Furthermore, if as a result of the common market workers suffered loss of employment, certain forms of aid were to be made available to them.

It is, therefore, within this politico–economic framework that the social policy provisions of the Treaty of Paris must be considered. A major difficulty in so doing arises from the need to determine the criterion upon which to select those treaty clauses which are to be discussed and this in turn reflects the difficulty of determining the precise meaning to be given to the word 'social' in such phrases as 'social well-being', 'social goals' and 'social policy'. In one sense, the whole treaty is social in objective in that the pursuit of peace and prosperity in Europe is an activity designed to promote social well-being. Today, however, the term 'social policy' is often given a more precise meaning. This can perhaps be more readily appreciated if the matter is considered for a moment in national terms. Although problems of definition abound, particularly over the matter of the boundary of social policy and its content, its core has normally been taken to consist of those activities promoted by public authorities which contribute directly to individual well-being. Unfortunately, this definition is increasingly becoming of limited value. In the first place, the boundary between policies which can be defined as directly promotional of indi- vidual welfare and the general activities of government is extremely arbitrary. To take one example, the promotion of individual health is dependent upon environmental health services, control of air pollution, transport systems and the like in addition to the provision of personal health services. Individual welfare can be both promoted and harmed by policies, notably those in the economic sphere, which are taken for economic, defence or political reasons. Furthermore, from the point of view of the individual, the definition has a great weakness in that it has traditionally excluded wage levels from consideration although, with the struggle to establish income policies, this drawback in social policy dis- cussion will be increasingly overcome. Finally, the definition ignores too readily the interplay between the polity and the economy in the pro- motion of individual well-being. It is particularly important to appreciate this factor which, of course, did not operate in the six founder members of the Community in precisely the same way. Very considerable differences continue to exist between them and between them and the new members in this respect. For a variety of political, historic and economic factors, the British approach to welfare has relied heavily upon the role of public authorities, whilst France and Germany have seen a function such as social security provision far more in the context of the industrial milieu. In consequence the term social policy can imply the wage and benefit return to labour, the range of governmental policies devoted to individual welfare together with the control exercised over other agents in such matters or a mixture of the two. It must be accepted that there is a good deal of overlap in definition and in functions and that the substance of social policy evolves over time. The critical element, however, is that of a policy consciously adopted to promote the welfare of human beings in a direct way, whether by central or local government, by firms or voluntary agencies. To argue, as is often done in the case of the European organizations, that their contribution to social well-being is through their creation of greater economic prosperity is tantamount to saying that they have no social policy. This requires the power to use resources for social ends. The social policy of the Communities, therefore, depends upon their ability to promote individual well-being either by direct acts of their own or by ensuring that other agents, such as states or firms, carry out policies for this purpose. It is in this sense that the work of the European organizations is considered.

In its recognition of the inter-relationship of broad social and economic ends there can be no question but that the Treaty of Paris is a socially responsible document. At this level there are three broad themes to be found in it. The first is that economic prosperity, greater employment opportunities and a rising standard of living go together, the second that the achievement of a rational productive system must be balanced by the need to safeguard the continuity of employment (Art. 2) and the third that a basic aim of the Community is to promote better conditions of living and of work for workers in each of the industries for which it is responsible so as to lead to their *'égalisation dans le progrès'* (Art. 3). Economic and social aims run in harness and are equally legitimate goals. A major weakness, however, results from the lack of fully capable procedures for their implementation so that to some degree they remain as aspirations rather than the basis of concrete policies. No instructions were given to the High Authority to enable it to contribute directly to a rising standard of living or to promote better living and working conditions, and such aims were therefore necessarily left heavily dependent upon interpretation by the institutions of the Community coupled with their willingness to use their general powers to pursue such ends with vigour. The conclusion must therefore be that, in so far as definite action is necessary to pursue such aims, the treaty left a great deal to those agents traditionally responsible, namely national governments and the industries themselves.

Certain aspects of these broad goals were, however, taken up in further detail and it is here that one finds the existence of powers which enabled the Community to share in organized activity of a social nature. The outstanding feature of the treaty, from this point of view, is its system of protection against unemployment. Much of the apprehension on the union side concerning the new Community related to the question of whether employment prospects would be improved or limited by it and the adoption by the Community of an adequate system of labour protection was therefore one means whereby acceptance was achieved. In particular it was anticipated that high-cost coal mines in Belgium and France would be compelled to reduce their labour forces and perhaps cease production altogether. Studies of comparative costs and prices (see Table 1.1) showed wide differences in which the average Belgian pithead

price of coal was twice that charged in West Germany as well as considerable variations between one coal field and another. Labour costs in
France and Belgium were particularly high. Any major readaptation
resulting from the introduction of a common market was thus likely to
fall on Belgium and France. Estimates suggested that perhaps thirty
thousand workers would become redundant in Belgium, especially in

Table 1.1
Comparative Efficiency and Costs in Belgium, France and West Germany, 1949 [28]

	Output per man shift (tons)	Labour Costs (US dollars per ton)	Total Operating Costs (US dollars per ton)	Estimated pithead price
Belgium	0·64	9·13	13·97	14·63
of which Liege	0·55	10·96	16·80	17·61
France (including Saar)	0·72	6·13	8·22	9·37
of which Nord	0·64	6·88	8·74	9·95
Cevennes	0·59	7·76	9·85	11·23
Saar	0·85	5·27	8·48	9·50
Dauphine	0·60	8·15	10·35	11·80
West Germany	1·03	3·76	6·66	7·19

Liege, and about fifty thousand in France, the majority in the Nord coal
field.[29] Thus the fear of unemployment resulting from the introduction
of the common market was the dominating social issue in 1951. This
required a social policy to protect the labour force from the task of
bearing the main cost of such introduction which, it was generally
assumed, would destroy the least efficient mines and firms or, as a
minimum, demand their fundamental reorganization and modernization.
Although a 'rational distribution of production' might benefit the Community at large there was doubt as to whether this was in fact compatible
with the responsibility to 'safeguard the continuity of employment'.[30]
Whilst statesmen might argue that the conception of the Community was
built on that of the welfare economy, others were suspicious of it as a
large-scale employers' agreement achieved at the expense of the living
standards of the workers. The fact that the treaty provided no direct
policy for wage improvement or employment, both of which remained
national responsibilities, meant that labour's fears were not groundless.
In the initial states an act of faith was required to accept the argument
that the condition of labour could improve through the acceptance of the
treaty system. After considerable debate, however, both the International
Federation of Christian Trade Unions (IFCTU) and the ICFTU approved the
notion of creating the Coal and Steel Community and their representatives
entered the national delegations which undertook the work of treaty
drafting[31] and continued to co-operate in the running of the Community's activities.

It is noticeable that, in contrast to the failure to specify the means to be used to improve the standard of living or the harmonization of the conditions of life, the provisions of the treaty to deal with problems of unemployment were precise and detailed. The treaty clearly accepted that 'the impact of such adjustments should not be borne by the workers and that their cost should be jointly financed'.[32] Such problems were covered in the first instance by Art. 23 of the transitional convention providing for certain action if firms were damaged in consequence of the setting-up of the common market. At the request of the government concerned, the High Authority was entitled to participate in studies of the possibilities of re-employment. Furthermore, it was entitled to receive governmental requests for grant aid from the ECSC towards the creation of new jobs for redundant workers, giving a preference to cases which could be attributed to the introduction of the common market. Additional forms of grant aid were devised to pay allowances to workers losing their jobs because of closures and having to wait for new employment or being temporarily laid off due to modernization, and to help pay for resettlement costs and vocational retraining when new jobs became necessary. Compensation to firms which would have to close down as a result of the introduction of the common market was also envisaged. The worker allowances and grants to firms put out of business had to be matched by the appropriate national government unless the Council authorized an exception. Similar long-term provisions were written into Art. 56 of the treaty, but when the time came to operate them it had become clear that the real difficulties facing the industries, and particularly coal, were likely to result less from the development of Community projects than from fundamental changes in energy markets. In consequence, in 1960 an amendment was made to Art. 56 which allowed for such aids to workers losing their jobs because of technical changes in the industries or because of fundamental changes in marketing conditions not directly attributable to the common market and subsequent allowances have always been made under this additional provision.

A further method of maintaining employment was given to the High Authority by Art. 58. This allowed it, after consultation with the consultative committee and with a concurring opinion from the Council, to establish a system of production quotas and to give special financial aid to firms in particular difficulties.

The system in general, and the functions of the High Authority in particular, thus recognized a direct responsibility to deal with problems of unemployment. In contrast, and despite the fears of employers concerning their costs and the wish of unions to see the Community work to equalize the labour return, wages and social charges only became of direct concern to the Community in exceptional circumstances.

Recommendations[33] might be made by the High Authority when a low wage level appeared to give an unfair competitive advantage, as would be the case if wages were abnormally low in comparison with those generally earned in the region or as a result of government decision. The possibility of using wages, or the financing of social security, or measures to deal with unemployment as means of providing a subsidy to the coal or steel industry was subjected to the same control as state aid and subsidies generally and a failure to conform to the recommendations of the High Authority could be penalized by fining (Art. 68). In the main, however, questions of wages and social benefits remained to be settled in traditional ways and the High Authority accepted no responsibility for them.

A significant contribution to social well-being has been made by the ECSC through its grant aid to housing schemes. Of this no mention can be found in the treaty. Art. 54 provides for the possibility of grants or loans to firms designed to contribute to their improved functioning and came to be used by the High Authority, with the unanimous support of the Council, in this way.

The principle of the free movement of labour was only partially accepted in the Treaty of Paris where it was limited to skilled workers (Art. 69). States agreed to remove any nationality restrictions for Community members preventing the employment of skilled workers anywhere within the Community frontiers, subject to basic limitations for reasons of health and public order. The definition of jobs and the appropriate qualifications suitable for recognition was left over to a later date, although members agreed to establish technical procedures to bring together offers of, and demand for, employment over the Community area as a whole. A further preference given in the treaty to the Community national was the acceptance by members of the obligation to facilitate the re-employment of workers from the coal and steel industries who did not possess such qualifications, an obvious means of cushioning the shock of the introduction of the common market should it be required, although likely to be limited in impact because of the notorious reluctance of miners to move. Of more practical significance was the recognition by states of the possible need to recruit foreign labour in order to obtain the expansion of which the treaty spoke and consequently to adapt their immigration rules and to remove discriminatory practices regarding pay and working conditions which would penalize such employment. One particular problem singled out for attention was the need to prevent social security measures forming a barrier to labour mobility. Finally, the treaty allowed for the continuance of special measures relating to frontier workers who formed a very considerable proportion of the labour force. These tentative moves towards mobility were left to the members for implementation. Their subsequent agreement

was required in order to surmount the welter of national laws, discriminatory practices, bilateral agreements and practical difficulties which might
act as an effective impediment to mobility and to express the degree to
which unions were prepared to accept the introduction of migrant labour.

Under Art. 55 the High Authority was bound to encourage technical
and economic research relating to the coal and steel industries including
questions of workers' safety. In order to do this it was obliged to organize
contacts among existing research organizations, to initiate and facilitate
the development of appropriate research work and to make the results
widely known. For these ends it was entitled to encourage joint financing,
to allot any gifts it might receive for this purpose and to make grants
from its levy income provided the Council approved.

In consultation with governments, employers, workers and other
interested persons, the High Authority was made responsible for the
collection of information necessary in order to take steps to improve the
living and working conditions of the labour force and was obliged, if so
requested by governments, to study the possibilities for the re-employment
of redundant labour. The right to call for such information was
independent of the Council or of member governments. The High
Authority was given the right to publish such work and, in view of the
paucity of material available at the time and its lack of comparability,
the significance of such studies should not be lightly dismissed.

The capacity of the High Authority to carry out its functions was
enhanced by its financial powers. These arose from the right to levy a
production tax, to contract loans, receive gifts and impose fines. The
purpose of the levy was to cover administrative expenses, non-repayable
readaptation aid, technical and economic research and to support the
provision of loans. The financial powers of the High Authority, although
not unlimited, were wide and formed a significant aspect of the treaty
enabling it to establish the importance of certain procedures, notably in
relation to benefits to the unemployed. One of its first priorities was to
set up a reserve fund against which it could borrow on the capital markets
or from institutions within the Community area and much of the
response of the High Authority to social and economic need was possible
because of its financial independence.[34] This was shown particularly
clearly in the coal crisis of the late 1950s when, although national
solutions were favoured by the Council, the High Authority had the
ability to grant aid certain Belgian mines and coal stockpiling in order
to ease adverse social consequences. The first guarantee operation of the
High Authority was to support a readaptation scheme approved under
Art. 23 of the transitional convention by which it contributed towards
new industrial installation in order to facilitate the re-employment of
workers in the Italian iron and steel industry.[35] Such financial arrangements conferred a considerable degree of independence but one must

remember that many of the objects for which the High Authority was entitled to raise money could not be adopted without prior approval of the Council. Nevertheless, it was the twin powers of being able both to exert control over the working of enterprises without reference to national governments and to raise funds which it was responsible for spending which formed the core of the supra-national character of the work of the High Authority and made it greater than a traditional organization for international co-operation. Through these powers, it possessed a true independence of action.

In practice, therefore, social policy consisted primarily of methods of compensation for economic change affecting workers' jobs in which the impact of the introduction of the common market was originally the major factor. The possibility of more fundamental economic action to maintain the continuity of employment, or of activities designed to promote better living and working conditions remained as promises for the future, whilst no direct control over wages and working conditions existed. In the meantime the national welfare structures remained relatively untouched and were clearly intended to continue to carry the main responsibility for direct measures of social improvement. The capacity to undertake studies, to call for information and to use financial resources in constructive ways provided the opportunity for work unspecified in the treaty itself. Ideologically, however, it was largely a defensive system quietening the fears of the timorous and enabling them to accept the new arrangements and to be willing to work within them.[36] It is difficult to argue that these powers were adequate fully to implement the broad social purposes the treaty claimed to further. Social policy is best viewed as an adjunct to the wider political and economic purposes of the treaty rather than as a central feature. The Community

> provides for action on behalf of labour solely as a condition or a consequence of its economic policy; it has neither a true social inspiration nor a social policy of its own . . . it can only contribute to social development without being responsible for it because its scope is restricted to the coal and steel industries, whereas wages and employment depend on general economic conditions in each country.[37]

This opinion of an independent observer is borne out by Paul Reuter's own account. In his study of the ECSC only five pages are devoted to social policy within the context of the ability of the High Authority to intervene in the operation of the market. He considered that it was neither necessary nor desirable to allow the High Authority responsibility for wages and social legislation as they affected the coal and steel industries. Its competence therefore had inevitably to be shared with states and unions.[38]

In practice the restriction of social responsibility to the workers of one industrial sector reinforced the concept of social policy as a function of its smoother working to concentrate the attention of the High Authority on the central issues of manpower and employment around which all its interests in the use, recruitment, training, wages and conditions of work of the labour force were developed. This concentration of interest was aided by, and in turn reinforced, the strong sense of the inter-relationship between economic and social developments which the treaty had expressed. The argument that the achievement of economic prosperity is itself a major tool in the pursuit of improved standards for the mass of the people and thus that social ends are served by economic progress was implicit in the early articles of the treaty. The High Authority, therefore, found itself arguing for social progress not always as an end in itself but as a means of achieving the economic purposes of the treaty.

It is this desire for the close interlinking of the Community's economic and social objectives, and the effective dovetailing of economic and social policy which animates the whole of the High Authority's work. Social progress is conditioned by economic progress. Only through a 'more rational distribution of production at a higher level of productivity' is it possible to ensure a lasting improvement in conditions generally. But, conversely, it is equally true to say that social progress determines economic progress. Terms of employment, vocational training, industrial safety are essential factors in any stepping up of productivity; the raising of workers real incomes creates the outlets necessary to an expanding production . . . On the other hand, there is no automatic correlation between economic and social progress. Specific social action is needed, therefore, to ensure that economic and technical progress actually is reflected in the improvement and levelling-up of living and working conditions for the workers in the Community industries.[39]

Table 1.2
ECSC Expenditure[40]
(m.u.a.)

I   *Loans for social purposes by 31 December 1970*

	Germany	France	Italy	Rest	Total	Percentage of total Community loans
Housing	64.3	21·6	14.2	34·1	137.3	13.0
Redevelopment	43·7	26·9	26·7	52·1	149·4	14·5
Readaptation	5·8	0·5	—	—	6.3	0·6
Research	1·4	0·6	0·2	0·8	3.0	0.3
Misc.	—	—	—	0.7	0.7	0.1
TOTAL	115·2	49·6	41·1	87·7	294·5 (approx.)	28·5

II   *Levy expenditure*

	1970	Estimate for 1974
Administration	18·0	18·0
Readaptation	26.0	41.0
Research	10.0	21.5

The belief in the inter-relationship of economic and social objectives, the responsibility for a partial sector of the economy only, the fact that it was by virtue of their role as workers that members of the coal and steel industries were distinguishable from the population as a whole, the long-established aim in Western Europe of trying to achieve better working conditions and the economic difficulties with which the coal industries were later confronted, all combined to produce an overwhelming pressure forcing the Community to focus upon the conditions of the workers in the coal and steel industries as the means by which to fulfil its obligation to promote the social well-being. The table demonstrates the scale of activity.

2 *The Social Impact of the Coal Crisis*

I The Declining Market

The opening of a common market in coal and steel was expected to bring fundamental, although largely unknown, changes since 'national markets had been characterised by a systematic attempt on the part of each state to favour its own producers to the detriment of others'.[1] It was not clear what effects the removal of such protection would have either on individual producers or on national situations themselves, although it was generally realized that certain older, high-cost mines needed either modernization or closure. Immediate preparations were covered by a convention to allow for the setting-up of the new institutions, the preliminary study of problems and the introduction of the perequation levy for coal. This tax, matched by comparable aid from the national governments of the high-cost mines, was intended for the reorganization necessary to establish the weaker units on a competitive basis.[2] During the transition period[3] special protective measures might be continued. The Belgian coal market as a whole received temporary insulation, which was later extended to 31 December 1962 because of the difficulties then being experienced and which resulted from fundamental changes in the demand for coal superimposed upon the uneconomic character of many of the Belgian pits. The Italian coal mines at Sulcis received perequation aid until 1955 for reorganization within the context of a programme acceptable to the High Authority, the Italian government and the Carbosarda Company.[4] Other transitional provisions allowed for the safeguarding of French coal production and the overall protection of the steel industry should such measures be necessary, for special protection for Luxembourg steel and for the continued maintenance of customs duties on Italian imports of coke and steel. The possibility of temporary, national subsidies was envisaged and these were used initially to help French briquetting firms, but the intention was for a gradual elimination of such aids and the integration of coal and steel production over the whole area. Within the context of such measures, the special forms of assistance to workers who lost their jobs because of the introduction of the common market and of Community aid to firms hit by it were laid down.

24

Until the latter part of the transition period the future for the coal and steel industries seemed secure. Shortly after the signature of the Treaty of Paris, the outbreak of the Korean War created an unexpected demand so that the basic need seemed to be to expand production and to make industry generally more competitive through the modernizing of existing plant whilst giving to uneconomic units a period of time in which to become competitive or go out of business without great hardship. A falling-off of demand in 1953 provoked some difficulty in marginal mines and led to the first attempt of the High Authority to operate a system of removal aid for certain French miners (see chapter 3). This, however, was no more than had been anticipated and the generally expansive economic environment brought the advantage that the period of the introduction of the common market could be completed with the minimum degree of inconvenience, the system become effective and a favourable psychological climate established. Since only a small number of firms, and thus of workers, were at first affected, economic integration apeared a relatively painless affair. On the other hand, the spur of the common market was correspondingly less effective and differing degrees of competitiveness tended to be reflected in the extent to which firms shared in the general expansion rather than in the wholesale elimination of the unfit.[5] Price differences at first remained considerable and in particular the expected, fundamental reorganization of the Belgian coal mining industry was delayed.[6] With the introduction of the common market for steel in the summer of 1954 and the favourable conditions of the next two years, the way seemed clear for the development of a new stage on the assumption that the immediate difficulties of introducing the new system were largely over. Subsidies for the coal industry in France were further reduced, a terminal date fixed for the operation of a price fixing scheme in the Netherlands and the perequation aid for Belgium re-examined with a view to its reduction.[7]

The decline in the fortunes of the coal industry which was becoming visible in 1957 provided an unexpected test of the treaty and of the strength of international decision taking. By now the coal industry was beginning to run into difficulties caused by the competition of cheaper, imported coal and of alternative forms of fuel, so that the European Parliament had already suggested that the High Authority should begin to frame the basic principles of a coal policy including future investment policies and manpower programmes.[8] By 1958 large unsold stocks were piling up at the pitheads, unemployment and short-time becoming frequent, especially in Belgium and Germany where recruitment was suspended or severely curtailed,[9] whilst the problems of the older mines could no longer be avoided. Far from being a temporary setback, it now appeared probable that future demand for coal would be permanently reduced and that the Community would become dependent upon imported fuel whether coal or oil.[10] Coal production dropped from 248 million tons (hard coal production) in 1957 to 227 million tons in 1962, 218 million tons in 1965 and 177 million tons in 1969.[11] Despite fluctuations in demand and thus in employment from year to year, the overall picture was one of decline. It became increasingly obvious that it was necessary for coal industries to make a permanent adjustment to a smaller share of the energy market and this problem called for a re-evaluation of the role of subsidies, the formulation of an energy policy for the Community and the introduction of measures to ease the immediate threat of unemployment through aid to stockpiling procedures and cash benefits to individuals. In the application of such policies, economic and social objectives marched hand in hand. Steel, too, by the early 1960s, began to find markets more difficult as underdeveloped countries began to establish mills of their own and alternative products, such as plastics, came on to the market. New techniques, greater attention to research and money for new investment became matters of increasing importance. These changes disclosed the weakness of the treaty structure and the inability of the High Authority to establish an effective international context within which the fundamental adjustments might be made. A new situation was beginning which demanded a significant reduction in the size of the coal industry, and to a lesser extent that of steel, improved efficiency in those units which were to remain in production and some consideration of an overall energy policy. These challenging circumstances demanded a reconsideration of Community thinking about subsidies which had in any case not yet been fully eliminated but were now seen as acquiring a new importance as a means of cushioning the much more drastic changes likely to be necessary in the long term. The treaty had been concerned to see their abolition as incompatible with the new competitive system, but the Community was now faced with the possibility that, without widespread protection, notably for coal, serious social dislocation would result. A new approach was required, involving reconsideration of eligibility for subsidy and its duration, the pursuit of a more dynamic policy of regional redevelopment to provide new forms of employment for the much larger number of people who would now be looking for jobs outside the coal and steel sector as well as efforts to ensure that a streamlined industry emerged from the troubles capable of holding its own in the new conditions. The concept of subsidy in the treaty, as a temporary measure confined to the Community industries themselves, was too narrow a one to meet the new situation effectively. Acceptance of the need for selective assistance in order to help with rationalization, redevelopment and safeguards for the labour force replaced the original view of the desirability of stringent prohibition of subsidies.[12]

Under these pressures the High Authority therefore began to formulate a fundamental energy policy, covering all types of fuel rather than simply coal to which it was legally restricted, which would attempt to forecast the future demands of the area, the extent to which they might be met by coal and the implications for the industry in terms of its future size, employment prospects and efficiency. The reluctance of the Council to consider Community solutions delayed the acceptance of such a policy which, when it came, was limited to an agreement on guiding lines. Thus, in default of an effective, comprehensive energy policy, the return to national subsidization of the collieries to prevent hardship seemed inevitable, and the High Authority, which had originally been directed to act with limited intervention, now sought to establish its position as the agent to approve and control the forms of aid to the coal industry of the Community which were becoming widespread.

Thus the declining market presented the first occasion upon which the members of the Community were faced with the question of how far they were in fact prepared to see the new machinery develop. If the immediate crisis posed the question of the capacity of the High Authority to formulate supra-national policies the future raised the issue of the ability to establish a Community energy policy, shaped if necessary by the available investment controls. Serious conflicts of opinion arose since members often still preferred to take national decisions of protection, largely of a short-term nature, and the powers of the High Authority were not strong enough for it to obtain more than limited success in its economic goals. There was, however, less disagreement on the importance of ensuring that workers did not bear the brunt of structural changes in the coal industry and it was found possible to revise Art. 56 to ensure this. In Parliament M. Malvesti drew attention to the changes experienced by the coal industry which were much greater than those envisaged as likely in 1950 and, far from being limited to individual firms, were placing the economic health of whole regions in jeopardy. Despite the inter-governmental conference on regional reconversion held in 1960, he concluded not only that the situation was beyond the competence of the treaty but that experience had shown that the treaty's assumption of geographical mobility amongst workers was too facile.[13]

> There was for the most part no real energy policy at all, or where there was it tended to be thrust into the background. This was possibly inevitable, in view of the speed with which the recent trends in the energy economy have developed and the fact that neither in the member countries nor in the Community itself were the general outlines for an energy policy worked out in time. The Community is therefore now faced [i.e. 1960] with a wide range of measures adopted at national level, mostly to meet the particular situation in the country concerned rather than the needs of the Community.[14]

Emergency measures, taken by national governments, to control imports or provide subsidies made their appearance. One of the earliest was a decision of the German government to provide special aid to the Ruhr coal fields by paying a tax-free shift bonus to underground workers as a means of limiting price increases – an act which caused the High Authority some concern as an unacceptable form of subsidy. A solution was ultimately reached whereby the German government's contribution to the pension and insurance funds for miners was reduced correspondingly, but the episode showed that, with internal pressures arising from the regional and social complications of the coal situation, governments needed to take immediate steps and these, in default of a previously agreed Community policy, were inevitably nationally angled and thus 'at variance with the spirit of the Treaty of Paris'[15] *Ex post facto* approval from the High Authority was often sought for such action whilst the executive was itself struggling to achieve agreement on the outlines of a Community-based policy within which helping measures could be rationalized.

II The Subsidy Problem

The question of the use of subsidy in relation to the Treaty of Paris had the effect of illuminating the financial burden, and thus by implication the philosophy, of social security for the mining industry. One effect of the introduction of the common market had been to stimulate interest in comparative production costs of coal, iron and steel within the Six, including the extent of variation of wages, social security benefits and indirect wage costs such as holiday pay, the length of the working week and bonuses. Since information on a standardized international basis did not exist, studies had to be put in train on a long-term basis, but the declining coal market raised certain problems in an acute and urgent form. One of these was the heavy burden of social security costs thrown upon the mining industry due to its long-established history of protection. The industrial importance of coal, combined with the hazardous and disagreeable conditions of work which its extraction imposed, meant that miners were one of the earliest groups to obtain social security protection, and their benefits are still partially provided through special schemes on terms generally more favourable than those offered to the working population as a whole. The creation of special, protective funds for miners in Germany goes well back into the nineteenth century, whilst France made old age insurance compulsory for miners in 1894. With the extension of social security cover miners have been partially assimilated into general social security schemes but not always for the same purposes in all Community countries. As a result of this historical development, social security for miners is a highly complex field in which the international comparison of benefits and costs is a dubious undertaking. The definition of mining occupations is not uniform, special schemes exist for some purposes and not others, financial arrangements are neither the same as those which exist generally nor do they differ from such patterns in a uniform way, varied administrative methods, including the use of semi-independent institutions, are in use. Effective international comparisons can really only be made on a benefit-by-benefit basis.[16] One of the main contributions of the High Authority was, therefore, in the studies it made of costs and benefits for Community miners as a basis for valid comparisons, but a good deal of controversy surrounded the question of the definitions used and of the significance to be attached to the results. In consequence the identification of the true social security costs which fall on the mining industry remains something of an open question. One major fact, however, stands out. The arduous and dangerous nature of the job has led to a widespread belief that elderly miners should be able to obtain long-term cash benefits over and above those generally available. This may mean the receipt of an old age pension at an earlier age, on more generous terms and at a higher rate, long-service bonuses payable even if work continues and eligibility for invalidity pensions on the basis of a favourable definition of invalidity to cover those exhausted by mining although still capable of lighter work. Thus miners in Belgium, France, Germany and the Netherlands have all been accustomed to more liberal treatment than their compatriots and it is in relation to long-term benefits that the major differences from the general working population exist. Studies revealed that the Belgian old age pension could be drawn at fifty-five years by underground workers who had contributed for twenty years and at sixty by other miners and an 'incapacity' pension existed for workers over forty. The general population, in contrast, was eligible for pension only at sixty-five in return for forty-five years of contribution, with the possibility of drawing a pension at sixty years of age. In Germany a miner could draw an old age pension at sixty after twenty-five years of contribution, a long-term bonus at fifty and compensation if he became unemployed at fifty-five. In France, too, retirement at fifty was possible after thirty years of contribution. In Luxembourg miners belonged to a scheme complementary to the general one and might draw a pension at fifty-five after thirty-five years' work in the mines, at fifty-eight after thirty years and at sixty after twenty years instead of the normal arrangement of a pension at sixty-five after forty years of contribution. The principle of a preferential retirement pension was adopted everywhere although the terms and contributions payable, the definition of retirement and the extent to which the special hardships of mining were taken into account varied from one country to another.[17]

Since social security was largely provided on an industrial basis, the declining importance of coal to the economy in the post-war world, the unattractiveness of the work to young people, the deliberate use of policies to encourage early retirement or to play down recruitment as a means of adjusting to falling manpower requirements led to an ageing labour force and an increased social burden which the industry found difficult to sustain. The retired and disabled had to be supported by schemes which were not receiving an adequate influx of the young and healthy so that heavy charges, in comparison with those borne by other industries, were becoming increasingly onerous. By 1960 a situation had been reached in France, Germany and Belgium in which there were more beneficiaries than subscribers in the miners' pension schemes.[18] The problem of social security therefore became a different one from that envisaged by the authors of the Treaty of Paris, who had been concerned to prevent changes in financing designed to give any one national industry an unfair advantage vis-à-vis the coal industries of the other members. In practice it was rather the question of the abnormally heavy charges carried by the mining employers in comparison with employers generally, and whilst the removal of this disproportionate burden seemed a way of increasing the market competitiveness of coal it was unclear whether the assumption of such charges by governments was an unlawful subsidy under the Treaty of Paris. From a domestic point of view, a solution to this problem raised fundamental questions concerning the purposes and financing of social security within the context of national social welfare institutions. Rather than merge miners' benefits into general schemes in order to pass part of the burden on to industry as a whole, governments more generally adopted some form of state aid. In the Netherlands a definite state contribution became payable, in Germany the government covered the deficit in miners' funds on an ex post facto basis whilst the French government used both a subsidy and a transfer of monies from the general social security schemes. In varying degrees, governments began to make themselves responsible for the amounts whereby social charges in coal mining exceeded those in industry as a whole. Unfortunately, from an international viewpoint, state contributions increased more in some countries than in others bringing increasingly glaring disparities especially when the greater aid was given in those countries which had the lower production costs,[19] and since the tenor of the Treaty of Paris was against artificial aids it was not easy for the High Authority to accept this trend with equanimity.

> The real trouble about such action is that once started there is no knowing where it will stop. Increased participation by a country in the cost of social security with the object of eliminating the additional burdens on coal further entails payments out of public monies direct to the wage earners. It comes as no surprise to the High Authority to find that the Governments are far from wishing to have nothing further to do with the level of coal and steel prices, despite the fact that they have relinquished their right to fix such prices direct. But it

has a duty of preserving a balance among the different industries of the Community, and that balance can be so preserved only if Government assistance is confined to the exceptional cases specifically provided for in the Treaty, and absolutely precluded from developing either into an illicit means of competition (pointless under boom conditions) or into a dislocating factor in the Common Market.[20]

To the High Authority, therefore, government aid with social security charges appeared at first as an indirect way of continuing to influence prices which could no longer be directly fixed, but under the mounting pressures of the coal crisis it had to adapt itself to the continuance of subsidy.

Meanwhile discussions were also proceeding on the twin problems of the common energy policy and the rules to determine the legality of subsidies generally with the Community structure. A Protocol of 21 April 1964 [21] marked the stage of an agreement upon the basis of a common policy which might serve as the context for national developments up to 1970. By this time it had been accepted that the radical changes in the market must mean a rationalization of coal production and steps to alleviate the very heavy charges, especially social security costs, falling on the coal industry which would require government contributions in order to restore coal's competitiveness. At the same time, it was important to work out the principles of such aid as a Community system in order to prevent the distortion of competition which would otherwise result.

The Protocol recognized the urgency of formulating an overall energy policy and the need to prevent problems being solved on a day-to-day basis by national decisions not necessarily in the best long-term interests of the Community coal industry and often difficult to co-ordinate. It nevertheless accepted the principle of subsidy in order to keep a cheap source of energy and did not suggest the alternative approach of high import duties. In turn, this document became the basis for High Authority proposals submitted to the Council at the end of 1964 designed to harmonize government aid to the Community's coal industry as special action under Art. 95. These were finally accepted by the Council as Decision 3/65 of 17 February 1965. Although originally intended to last only until 31 December 1967, it was already clear later in the year that such a lapse would be premature and that more rethinking about how to aid coal would be necessary. The decision was ultimately replaced by Decision 3/71/ECSC of 22 December 1970 which continued the Community system of intervention through members for support of coal and contained a new emphasis upon the need to fit in with regional programmes.[22]

The 1965 agreement was based upon the principle that, whilst state aids were normally incompatible with Art. 4 (c) of the treaty, nevertheless a system of Community-organized assistance would be lawful since the Community was in a situation unforeseen by the treaty and therefore one which required regulation by Art. 95 (1). Although rationalization of mines was necessary, heavy costs would be incurred in the meantime which would prove too much for individual firms themselves to carry and therefore a temporary public subsidy was the only solution. Provided such subsidies met the requirements of Community rules then Art. 4 (c) was considered to be inapplicable. Community criteria were established to judge whether assistance was in fact in the common interest and only given on the scale necessary; prior High Authority approval had to be obtained whilst the executive was given powers of inspection and intervention to ensure the correct use of subsidies. Should it decide that the aid was such as to distort competition then it had the right to address a binding recommendation to the government concerned.

Under this system a wide range of measures became eligible for state aid under the Community rules. Activities designed to introduce mechanization, to concentrate pits, improve mine safety or to recruit and train personnel, to cushion the closure or contraction of particular collieries which led to expenses such as premature retirement pensions or compensation for loss of free coal or to help with the costs connected with actual closure operations were included. Temporary help, normally for one year, was permitted to enable closures of mines to be staggered so as not to cause too great an economic or social disturbance to any area. Social security costs, too, were included in the system whenever abnormal charges resulted from a fall in the number of active miners and a proportionate increase in the number of beneficiaries. Where this relationship was different from that appertaining in other industries, state intervention on the basis of an agreed formula to produce an equalization of the burden was to be approved and considered compatible with Art. 68 (5).[23] In practice about 90 per cent of subsidies granted took the form of social security aid [24] thus suggesting that there was a real need to spread the cost more widely over the economy or to stabilize the colliery labour force on a more typical age structure by the recruitment of younger workers.

In fact social security costs proved but one illustration of a wider issue. As studies demonstrated the importance of all indirect labour costs [25] and their tendency to rise more quickly than wages, the original preoccupation with wage levels as a competitive factor began to appear insufficiently sophisticated. The fears of wage-cutting were overtaken by an appreciation of the need to understand labour costs more fully, but the acceptance of subsidy meant that these did not have to be considered as an issue of practical policy at Community level. Moreover, since help with social security costs was largely necessitated by the problem of pensions, there seemed no reason why it should not continue beyond the period of drastic reductions in production. Subsidies designed to aid rationalization and to make mining more competitive were considered as temporary aids intended to decline as time went by, but this expectation was not fulfilled. Total Community aids under Arts. 3, 4 and 5 of Decision 3/65 were 81·6 million units of account in 1965, 163·7 million units in 1966, 352·3 million units in 1967 and 427·7 million units in 1968 [26] whilst the increase in government contributions to social security schemes continued.[27] The importance of social charges is suggested by the following table. The increase in governmental subsidies to social security costs allied with declining production is shown in Table 2.2 at the end of the chapter.

Table 2.1
Trend in Employers' Total Hourly Expenses and in Indirect Labour Costs Alone for Underground and Surface Workers in the Coal Industry [28]
(1954 = 100)

	Employers' total expenses	Indirect labour costs	Employers' total expenses	Indirect labour costs
	Germany		*Belgium*	
1955	109·0	106·1	103·7	110·3
1965	228·0	239·0	213·1	268·8
	France		*Netherlands*	
1955	110·4	113·7	110·9	111·9
1966	273·8	312·2	246·5	227·4

Within the context of these general measures, special attention had to be paid to the difficulties of the Belgian coal industry. It was known at the time of signature of the Paris Treaty that neither of her coal basins, and particularly the Borinage, was any longer efficient. In consequence the general provisions concerning gradual elimination of subsidy were supported by special arrangements to allow her to protect her markets and prices from the full rigours of the common-market system as well as to receive assistance from the perequation levy.[29] This was intended to decline in value and was given as part of a broader governmental scheme for reorganization. The total Belgian plan included an overhaul of pits suitable for integration and the gradual closing of those incapable of adequate improvement with the aid of subsidy from both the Belgian government and the High Authority. However, by a special decision of the Council,[30] the Community waived the normal obligation of the government concerned to contribute equally to readjustment arrange-ments and allowed the High Authority to be fully responsible for the help given to over a thousand workers as a result of the closing of certain pits in the Borinage.

Despite attempts to use the subsidy scheme more selectively from 1955 onwards, under encouragement from the High Authority, the ending of the transitional period did not bring the hoped-for improvements in the Belgian coal industry which by now was feeling the effects of the general coal crisis with particular severity. The treaty structure made the further continuation of the Belgian subsidy policy dependent upon agreement with the High Authority on the acceptability of the Belgian plans for reorganization,[31] and arrangements had to be made at a time when governments generally were taking protective action against imported fuels. Thus the special programme of pit closures which began in Belgium with support from the High Authority had to be matched by special restrictions on the import of coal. Despite such measures, the situation continued to be difficult, being characterized by unsold stocks, short-time working [32] and rising social tension.

As early as 1956, in its Memorandum on the Definition of the General Objectives, the High Authority had given its view that continuity of employment in the coal mining industry should be a major objective [33] for which a stockpiling policy should be used if necessary. In April 1958 it asked the Council to agree, under Art. 53 (b), to the introduction of financial arrangements designed to enable stocks to be held at the pit-heads. Despite considerable negotiation, it was not until October that the Council accepted a scheme, under Art. 95 (1), for a temporary system of High Authority aid for stockpiling where continuity of employment was threatened. Further measures suggested by the High Authority included the need to avoid short-time whenever possible through plans such as the rearrangement of holidays or the encouragement of those who could get other jobs to leave and the grant of special allowances to those who had to work short-time besides the introduction of special aid to help close down uneconomic pits. During September and October 1958 the Council agreed to temporary measures, based on Art. 95 (1) of the treaty, designed to allow the High Authority to use its own funds to aid stockpiling, and discussions between the executive and the Council explored the possibilities of curtailing production, improving consumption and controlling imports on agreed principles. [34] Such preventive, and often indirect, measures proved inadequate and the High Authority began to consider more direct forms of action.

During the winter the situation refused to improve. The Council agreed to maintain the system of High Authority aid for stockpiling, and import restrictions continued to be authorized, but by February 1959 the High Authority had concluded that the time for indirect measures had passed and that it was necessary for it to play a more effective role in the hope of more long-lasting and radical solutions for the coal industry. It announced on 29 February [35] that it was considering the question of using Arts. 58 (a state of manifest crisis) and 74, and discussions on this point continued with members and with the Council. On 25 March the Council agreed to a special, temporary grant, under Art. 95 (1), to assist Belgian mineworkers put on short-time payable up to a maximum of nine days within the same month and at a rate of 20 per cent of the workers' daily wage with the aim of trying to keep the income of those on short-time as near as possible to their full-time level. [36] The following month the High Authority sent directly to governments its draft plan to deal with the coal crisis based upon the need to curtail imports, reduce production on a selective basis, prevent further stockpiling and extend to the whole Community the measures applicable in Belgium to supplement the wages of those on short-time. The proposals were the culmination of eighteen months' work by the High Authority designed to deal with the problem as a crisis situation demanding Community solutions, but at the Council meeting of 14 May 1959 they failed to obtain majority acceptance. 'The most important factor was that national solutions were preferred to Community ones.' [37] The Council did agree, however, to further emergency measures to help the Belgian situation. These included the right of the Belgian government to subsidize coal prices,[38] further aid under Art. 95 (1) for short-time workers and High Authority aid under Art. 23 of the convention to permit the staggered closure of Belgian mines affected by the reorganization schemes during the period up to June 1961.[39] This readjustment aid included the payment of wages to workers in pits scheduled for closure provided certain conditions laid down by the High Authority, designed to provide it with more effective control, were accepted.[40] In June grant aid to those on short-time was further extended up to 30 September 1959. Meanwhile the High Authority and the Belgian government formulated a programme for the Belgian coal industry and the Council agreed to allow further subsidies on Belgian coal. A total ceiling of 7·5 million units of account was added to the aid to be provided under Art. 23 of the convention for those being maintained at uneconomic pits. In November the Council had to discuss yet again the extension of the special temporary allowance to mineworkers in Belgium as well as the proposed revision of Art. 56 of the treaty which was also running into difficulties.

III Cash Benefits for Miners

The key to the treaty system of protection for workers' employment lay in its 'readaptation' arrangements. It will be recalled that Art. 23 of the convention was designed to provide various forms of help to those damaged by the introduction of the common market, whilst Art. 56 of the treaty perpetuated the assistance provided its need was demanded by the introduction of technical processes or new equipment. Art. 23 was due to expire on 9 February 1960 but long before then it was clear that the employment problems resulting from the difficulties of the coal industry would not fall within the context of Art. 56 which was too narrowly drawn for these new circumstances. Some expansion of the article was required in order to cover problems of loss of work due to the contracting market and the structural changes taking place in the industry which appeared likely to continue.

Amendments to the treaty could be made in one of two ways. Under

Art. 95 it was possible to amend the rules under which the High Authority operated if unforeseen difficulties occurred in the execution of the treaty or if profound changes in the economic or technical conditions were experienced and provided the amendments did not lead to any fundamental change in the basic objectives or the structure of the Community. Such an amendment had to be proposed jointly by the High Authority and the Council acting on a five-sixths majority, examined by the Court and approved by the Assembly on a majority of three-quarters of the votes cast representing a two-thirds majority of the total membership. This came to be known as the 'minor revision' procedure and permitted revision of the treaty by the action of Community institutions only but provided all four were in accord.[41] This method was utilized for the broadening of Art. 56 since it was becoming clear during 1957 that a change would be necessary if the Community was to be able to help during the closure of more pits which by now was clearly foreshadowed.[42] In February 1958 the matter was raised officially in the European Parliament and a draft proposal sent to the Council in July 1959. Some governments felt dubious about committing themselves to a large-scale obligation for an indefinite future and it was, therefore, only an emasculated version which emerged from the Council in the autumn. The new suggestion allowed for the continuance of help to the workers of the coal industry if such help was necessitated by changes in market conditions but for a limited period of three years. Grant aid to industries was also covered. The Court of Justice, however, ruled the proposal to be out of order on the grounds of wide drafting, its application to the coal industry only and its limited validity. Further negotiations, strongly backed by Parliament, were therefore undertaken which resulted in a new draft proposal emerging from the Council meeting on 26 January 1960 by a five-sixths majority vote. This proved acceptable to the Court, was approved by the necessary majority in Parliament on 29 March and became section 2 of Art. 56.[43] It began to be used by the High Authority from November 1960. It allowed for aid to all sectors of industry covered by the treaty, was to remain in force for the full length of time of the treaty and covered the financing of new activities and conversions and the payment of four types of assistance to workers when such aid was necessitated by structural change.

By the middle of 1959 the situation in Belgium had become so grave that the Belgian government could no longer wait for the Community to agree to an overall reform plan. On 3 November she informed the High Authority that she intended to invoke Art. 37, dealing with the action of the executive or failure to act which was creating fundamental disturbances in the economy. This led to an agreement based on the need for a radically revised reorganization scheme for the Belgian coal industry, its partial isolation from the rest of the Community and from external competition.[44] It was accepted that the Belgian dilemma arose because of the importance of the coal industry to the Belgian economy, accounting for 12 per cent of gross national profit and 10 per cent of the labour force, coupled with the fall in the demand for coal and the social dislocations likely to occur should a rapid programme of pit closures be put into operation. It seemed therefore possible that it would be necessary to continue to operate uncompetitive mines indefinitely. Whilst the High Authority and Belgium agreed to a phased reduction of output of more radical nature than hitherto contemplated, the need for the continuation of substantial aid for humanitarian reasons was also accepted. Belgium agreed to put forward her more drastic proposals for the reduction of the coal industry by 1 May 1960 and in the meantime was allowed to limit imports from both the rest of the Community and elsewhere. She agreed to inform the High Authority of the measures taken and to limit them if the High Authority considered them too severe and likely to harm the Community itself.

In December the fear of disturbances in Belgium was raised in the Council and a further extension, up to 31 December 1959, of financial aid to short-timers was agreed. At the same time the possibility of continuing to pay this aid during 1960 was discussed. Although the Council accepted that it would be desirable, it also felt that it would have to be on a descending scale 'since 30 September 1960 had been put forward as the final date for all Community assistance to short-time workers'.[45] In the New Year the Council agreed to the revised draft of Art. 56, approved the memorandum from the High Authority on the Co-ordination of Energy Policy and accepted the details of the second scheme for payments to those Belgian miners on short-time. A maximum of three million units of account was allocated for the period from 1 January to 30 September 1960 for aid of up to 20 per cent of the daily wage for short-time working after the second day of short-time in any calendar month, the maximum number of eligible days being eight in January falling to four in September. The allowances were exempt from tax or from consideration when determining social security contributions.[46] At the request of the Belgian government, her coal industry continued to be discussed by the Council throughout the year, notably in October and November 1960 and January 1961. Subsidies, subject to a production ceiling, were kept and the renewal of the ECSC allowance on a sliding scale accepted up to a maximum of 1·3 million units. This was paid to Belgian miners from January to December 1961 [47] on the grounds that, although short-time working had fallen, some pits were still badly affected. The amounts paid out to short-time workers were in fact small in 1961.

The coal crisis therefore had a number of tangible results on the social side. Politically, it is generally accounted a failure in that it demonstrated the unwillingness of members to allow the evolution of High Authority policies to deal with unforeseen problems, which they preferred to continue to control themselves. The long discussions did, however, lead to the ultimate formulation of common rules for state aids which included a partial change in the financial arrangements for social security benefits. These had the general effect of moving provision away from separate, industrially based schemes towards more widely spread community responsibility. A directly obvious result was the amendment of Art. 56 in order to allow the High Authority to deal with a wider set of circumstances than hitherto, not only during the immediate crisis but for the indefinite future. Finally, the High Authority contributed financially to various forms of cash benefit received by the workers and the system proved sufficiently flexible to allow for the payment of aid to those on short-time. The experience must, therefore, be rated as one in which the Community system demonstrated its ability to react positively to human need.

Table 2.2

Assistance with Disproportionately High Social Security Costs in Accordance with Art. 2 (2) of Decision 3/65 [48]

	Amount (m.u.a.)			Amount per ton u.a.			Percentage increases in total expenditure	
	1965	1966	1967	1965	1966	1967	1966/65	1967/66
Germany	529·4	568·1	642·5	3·76	4·33	5·22	7·3	13·1
Belgium	110·2	117·4	128·3	5·57	6·71	7·97	6·6	9·2
France	249·2	270·8	297·1	4·86	5·35	6·05	8·7	9·7
Netherlands	9·9	21·0	21·0	0·85	2·04	2·33	111·1	0
Community	902·9	977·3	1088·9	4·04	4·67	5·52	8·2	11·4

	Production in million tons			Percentage decline in production	
Germany	140·6	131·3	123·0	− 6·6	− 6·3
Belgium	19·8	17·5	16·1	−11·6	− 8·0
France	51·3	50·3	49·0	− 2·0	− 2·6
Netherlands	11·7	10·3	9·0	−12·0	−12·6
Community	223·4	209·4	197·1	− 6·3	− 5·9

3 Protection against Unemployment

I Area Redevelopment

The debate on the proposal to introduce the Coal and Steel Community made plain that labour support would be necessary to reach the objectives of economic efficiency and rational distribution of production. A system deliberately designed to achieve such aims had thus to devise measures to cushion their anticipated consequences in order to minimize the conflict between the demands of technical change and the human need for continuity and stability of employment. 'There is nothing more important for the future of the European economy than to overcome this contradiction between the need for stability of employment and the demands of progress.'[1] Since, however, it is a good deal easier to argue in theory that the maintenance of out-of-date methods of production is harmful to the workers' standard of living than to convince those who are actually made redundant of its truth, a great deal was bound to depend upon the effectiveness of the arrangements actually made. It will be remembered that the Treaty of Paris contained specific provisions to compensate workers for the loss of employment resulting from the creation of the common market and to enable the High Authority to help industry create more jobs. In these ways the ECSC was a social system intended to buffer the worker against the responsibility of bearing the cost of changes and to win his acceptance of them.

Although direct aid to workers was important, the High Authority was increasingly led to consider the creation of alternative job opportunities as a more constructive means of protection. It was thus drawn into the general process of the economic development of the regions of heavy industry: 'finally, readaptation aids are becoming increasingly merged into reconversion work so that they are developing beyond the simple function of providing unemployment benefit to become one determinant of regional re-awakening'.[2] This experience bore fruit in the broader clauses of the Treaty of Rome, notably in the ability of the social fund to deal with unemployment however caused and the recognition of regional development needs. The later document, therefore, reflected an acceptance of the wider view that protection against unemployment is often best served by measures to create jobs in particular districts, to provide training facilities and resettlement grants so that workers may turn the processes of change to their advantage.

Applications for readaptation aid under the transitional convention made a slow start. An explanation can be found in buoyant economic conditions which cushioned the less efficient producers from the effects of greater competition and to the unfamiliarity of the system of grant aid. It was not until March 1954 that the High Authority took its first decision to contribute towards a readaptation scheme [3] and 1958 before work was being done on any scale. However, when Art. 23 expired on 9 February 1960 the High Authority had granted 42,518 million units of account towards help given to 115,085 workers of whom 80 per cent were miners.[4] Some examples of the type of project aided with redevelopment loans, the growth of readaptation aid, its various forms and destination by country and industry will be found in tables 3.1–3.4 at the end of the chapter.

It was perhaps unfortunate that the first scheme accepted by the High Authority had, as its major objective, one which rapidly came to be thought of as a second best. It was an application from the French government for aid to provide facilities for the transfer of five thousand miners from the Centre-Midi to work in the coal fields of Lorraine or to be absorbed there in other types of work, if necessary after retraining. The project was to be phased over a three-year period at a cost of one milliard francs to be shared equally between the Community and the French government [5] and consisted of a reinstallation grant [6] and removal costs for each miner who transferred. Extensive study of the project was undertaken by the French government, Les Charbonnages de France, the High Authority and union representatives; local committees representing workers and management were set up to supervise the operations, which were co-ordinated by a central office in Paris upon which the High Authority was represented. The French government additionally requested a loan to enable it to begin a building programme in Lorraine for the families who would be coming in.[7]

The ground was carefully prepared.[8] Information about the new jobs and allowances was issued by Les Charbonnages de France in April 1954 to men working in the mines of Aquitaine, Cevennes and Provence, whilst parties of workers were sent to Lorraine to survey the position and report back to their fellows. The first departures took place in May, but by the beginning of 1955, only 258 men had volunteered to move, only 145 had actually gone and during the life of the scheme but 600 out of the hoped for 5,000 had transferred.

The reasons for this relative failure were complex. It seems clear, however, that the reluctance of the miners to leave their home environment, a pleasant climate and side-line jobs was reinforced by fears of local business men over loss of trade as well as by anti-Community propaganda concerning renewed deportation. The High Authority reacted strongly to this experience from which it derived two important lessons for the future. Firstly, that in any further scheme transfers should be kept in line with the availability of housing since the lack of accommodation in the reception area had been a major impediment to the willingness to move and it was only after the scheme had begun that building for the newcomers was stepped up. Secondly, and more importantly, that the deep reluctance of the miners to leave, even at the price of unemployment, made schemes to provide jobs on the spot inherently more promising. When, therefore, it appeared probable later in 1955 that other miners in the Centre-Midi would be laid off, cash allowances were also made available to those unwilling to move, although on rather different terms than those offered to migrants, whilst the High Authority and the French government entered into discussions concerning the possibility of creating local employment. Readaptation schemes increasingly accepted that it was unwise to assume geographical mobility and were better based on plans to develop areas.[9]

The new approach implied a definite broadening of the scope of the High Authority's activities. Whilst the Treaty of Paris gave it limited opportunity to help in job creation, the need for massive redevelopment of the regions of heavy industry and for maintaining their economic life had not been foreseen. Severe contractions gave rise to problems of economic ill-health affecting the general prosperity of a whole region through the cumulative loss of economic momentum. Recognition of the existence of a variety of problems, including the unattractiveness of an out-of-date environment to new firms, the inheritance of decay, the high proportion of older workers who could no longer find work and the general depression of the market for new products all stimulated acceptance of the need for active, and possibly long-term, measures of regeneration to try to maintain the general standard of well-being at a level comparable with that of expanding cities.

> From the information which is now available it seems that the coal and steel industries must make further efforts of adaptation in the next four or five years. In the coal fields, production is still noticeably declining and the number of unemployed remains considerable. The iron ore mines continue to contract. Whilst it is more difficult to make precise estimates for the future in steel, it is certain that there will be further reductions in employment.[10]

Although there is no specific development policy laid down in the Treaty of Paris, the Community's responsibility for the coal and steel industries made it impossible for it to ignore the implications of industrial contraction for the areas where they were situated. The objectives laid down in Art. 2 would need a very narrow interpretation if no consideration were to be given to the impact of the changes of economic fortunes in coal and steel on areas which have been heavily dependent upon them. The expansion of Art. 56 made it clear that the Community recognized some responsibility to help to create alternative forms of employment for those no longer employed in the coal and steel industries through enabling it to participate in national redevelopment schemes, but the initiative for such policies and for drawing on the Community depended upon national action. Thus Art. 46 (4) allowed the Authority, at the request of the government concerned, to participate in the study of re-employment possibilities for redundant labour and Art. 56 permitted it to support projects to provide new work by means of loans or guarantees thereof. This could, however, only be done on governmental request and, in the case of activities which were not within the coal and steel industries, had also to receive the support of the Council. The national government thus played a key role at all stages both in initiating studies and requests for aid, in being willing to bear half the cost of projects under Art. 56 and in being responsible for seeing that regional projects got going on approved lines. In addition, the High Authority could call upon its more general powers of consultation and information seeking under Art. 46 and of research to indicate fields in which it considered action to be desirable.

The realization that 'on-the-spot' readaptation was likely to prove more effective led naturally on to interest in general economic strategy, to the possibility of introducing new forms of industry into older areas and to the need to maintain their overall standards at levels comparable with expanding areas elsewhere. The increased interest in regional policies led to a growing volume of applications for financial aid for development schemes as part of an overall regional plan and this forced the High Authority to consider its policy towards industrial regeneration, to formulate the part it could play successfully in view of its limited responsibilites (for Art. 56 [2a] defines the boundaries of its regional aid), and to determine how best to influence schemes in accordance with its own views. In 1959 the Belgian government embarked on regional development plans which included coal field areas and requested the High Authority to participate in studies of the Borinage area to enable effective plans to be worked out with a view to its integration into the common market, bearing in mind the type of development intended in northern France.[11] Meanwhile the creation of the EEC, by recognizing the importance of regional development as a whole, accentuated the need to view the future of the coal and steel industries in a wider context and made it more urgent to formulate the role of both national and international agencies in this respect.

On 31 July 1959[12] the Council and the High Authority jointly decided to call an inter-governmental conference to study the economic and social problems of these regions and this heralded a step towards more active regional policies at the international level. Considerable preparatory work was undertaken by officials from the High Authority, the EEC, the European Investment Bank, created under Art. 129 of the Rome Treaty and especially concerned with regional development projects, representatives from governments, including the United Kingdom, and of the Council of Ministers. The conference met from 27 September to 1 October 1960. Each national delegation included civil servants and representatives of both employers' and workers' organizations. Observers from the International Labour Organization (ILO), Austria and the United States also attended, together with outside experts. The conference examined in depth substantive issues connected with redevelopment problems on the basis of previous experiences in dealing with them and discussed the legislative measures open to governments to create new activities as well as the means of intervention available to European institutions and the forms of co-operation between these different levels of authority. It emphasized the need to prevent the economic and social decay of an area rather than to wait until it was impoverished and morale low and only then to consider the question of its reactivation, thus establishing a basic common principle over the whole territory of the member countries in favour of the creation of new jobs on the spot and at an early stage.

The conference was significant in that it provided a Community dimension for regional problems. It pointed to the value of the interchange of ideas and experience in a relatively new field of endeavour and made it easier to consider as a whole the needs of areas which are geographically coherent although divided by national frontiers. By formulating its belief in the reanimation of decaying areas it established the basis for national policies and for the work of the European institutions. Finally, it agreed that the Communities should assist in planning and financing redevelopment projects and thus implied their necessary involvement in the general economic prosperity of a region. Following the conference, the High Authority formulated its 'Guiding Principles for Dealing with Problems in Connection with Industrial Redevelopment of Areas Affected by Pit Closures' which was discussed by the Council on 4 December 1961. Whilst this memorandum accepted that governments retained the main responsibility for regional development and for the selection of means for any particular case, it stressed the need to strengthen the forms of co-operation between the European institutions in order to deal more effectively with applications for aid and for involving governments and outside experts in its work of studying and preparing redevelopment operations. This meant consultation prior to practical action as well as agreements between ECSC and EEC on the sharing of the cost of European aid in particular schemes.[13] A joint working party, representing the High Authority, the Commission and the

European Investment Bank (EIB) subsequently examined all redevelopment schemes for which governments sought aid from the European institutions.

Since national governments remained the operative units for regional planning and aid, it was not only important that the High Authority remained in close contact with them in order to formulate its own policies but it implied that a valuable function for it to perform was to encourage the exchange of ideas and experience at inter-governmental level. The main agency created for these purposes was the committee of national experts set up in 1961 to provide the High Authority with continuing advice on industrial redevelopment[14] and to ensure that all members were associated with its work. It was a specific function to remain in touch with official and industrial circles dealing with redevelopment in individual countries and to supply national and local authorities and prospective investors with relevant material. Through its ability to offer advice and appraisal of development operations it could encourage the formulation of properly thought-out schemes which required High Authority aid, whilst also acting as a depository of information and a general clearing house for the exchange of ideas.

The committee prepared a number of reports including work on the socio-economic structure of mining and steel-making areas, the location and preparation of industrial sites and their relation to social infrastructure, on the role of industrial building, the type of new production lines likely to be successful in redevelopment areas and on agencies involved in regional redevelopment.[15] In this way it hoped to establish certain general principles which could be used as guiding lines for redevelopment anywhere in the Community.[16]

The High Authority, however, also participated in national planning activities. An example is the Belgian national steering committee on coalfield redevelopment problems representing ministries and including a representative from the ECSC. The committee not only studied development in the coal fields but performed a co-ordinating function inside Belgium itself.[17] Many agencies are necessarily involved in redevelopment schemes and the co-ordination of their work is an essential requirement of effective working. If people can be involved in planning discussion from the start this very knowledge can help the morale of the labour force and encourage firms to remain in, or enter, an area. The phasing of activities, too, can be important so that industry has the services it requires from the start. Such planning requires detailed knowledge of individual areas and their potentiality. It is often at the regional level itself that work, particularly the preliminary studies, is most effective. The needs of each area must be assessed and catered for,[18] the contribution of each agency determined and the phasing of operations carefully timed. Planning and execution can be seen as two stages in the same operation and, in both, the High Authority found a part. Some of its studies appear to have contributed to the formation of local working committees responsible for effective co-ordination of the work of different agencies and it played an active part in the work of such organizations.[19] In such activity it was for the High Authority to use both its influence and its financial power to affect the content and outcome of development schemes.

The High Authority was thus drawn into activity which was originally nationally based. Industrial redevelopment became a task to be shared by national and international authorities with the consequent need for machinery to co-ordinate the work involved and for the High Authority to determine its policy objectives. It has already been noted that its interest turned to the possibility of creating new jobs, whether in the coal and steel industry or otherwise, not all of which it would be practicable to fill with redundant miners or steel workers, but its policy was based on the belief that, wherever possible, new work must be taken to the worker rather than that he should be expected to move and that, in consequence, it had to play a role in the general support of the economy of the coal and steel regions in order to make this possible.[20]

> Miners and steel workers are as a rule most unwilling to leave their own areas. The object of redevelopment . . . is to make it possible for discharged workers to continue earning a living in the localities to which they are accustomed.
> The true function of redevelopment is, however, something very much wider than merely eking out readaptation where this is not in itself sufficient. Redevelopment transcends rather than supplements readaptation: it operates to the benefit not merely of ECSC workers but of the whole working population of the area concerned, since by ensuring that an enterprise closing its doors is replaced by one or more other concerns it prevents the whole district from going economically downhill.
> Redevelopment may be expected as time goes on to extend well beyond the sphere of social policy as such, and to become a major factor in industrial development.[21]

As experience was gained, the operations helped by the Authority became more variable, with the consequence that it was increasingly concerned with the well-being of a region as a whole. Additionally, it was committed to a belief in early planning and preventive action lest a district lost its economic momentum, and considered that this should be done thoroughly from the start in that plans to deal with the full range of redundancies rather than immediate problems alone tended to be more satisfactory. It believed that workers should be trained for new work prior to, or immediately on, discharge rather than left to experience a period of unemployment damaging to morale, destructive of their attractiveness to a new employer and their retraining capacity and which encouraged the younger and keener workers to migrate.[22] Preventive action suggested, too, the need to attract new industries in advance of pit or industrial closures at least in order to forestall economic decline and to phase pit closures and new openings together. Earlier and more sensitive planning necessitates a systematic approach to ensure the proper phasing of different types of industrial development, the successful location of employment opportunities and the interlocking of the necessary services. The High Authority was much attracted by the belief that the development of infra-structure and key activities in a region could themselves attract investment to a declining region and its help to the mining areas was often given with this consideration in mind.

A major aspect of the work was the sponsorship of studies in depth of the needs of particular areas, notably the large industrial basins, both as a preliminary to their redevelopment and as a means of building up knowledge of past arrangements so that decisions fundamental to successful redevelopment might become systematized and utilized by those involved and operations become progressively smoother in consequence. Studies of both particular problems and areas were sponsored by the committee of national experts and carried out by independent institutions with financial aid.[23] Small and medium-sized firms and the self-employed find it particularly difficult to assess the likely profitability of new lines or their chances of making a success in a redevelopment area and require material upon which to make a reasoned decision. A study was begun in 1962 of these problems with the object of helping such small units avoid mistaken decisions and thereby helping to prevent the occurrence of future redevelopment problems.[24] The transmission of accumulated material concerning the factors affecting the location of new industrial estates and the provision of necessary services, the balance of various activities or the phasing of development between areas, governments, financial institutions and firms interested in going into development areas became a significant function for the High Authority to perform. It was associated with a deliberate attempt to publicize policies and events in the belief that knowledge about redevelopment plans should be widely diffused among, and their importance understood by, the general population. Thus the 1960 conference was followed by a series of discussions with union officials and its findings referred to the consultative committee for debate, whilst in March a conference for the mayors of mining and steel towns was held to discuss the possibility of preparing advance plans, and the environmental improvements necessary to make such cities attractive to new industry and its workers.[25]

The first financial aid was provided in 1961 when firms in Belgium and France received loans on favourable terms which included a loan of 365,000 new French francs at 3¼ per cent to provide eighty jobs for mineworkers unemployed due to closure at Champagnac, but it was not until 1965 that the volume of assistance became substantial with help to the Liege area. This took the form of a credit valued at seven million florins from a loan recently raised in the Netherlands to create 470 new jobs in iron and steel and of 115 million Belgian francs for the *Societé provinciale d'industrialisation*.[26] The following year Belgium received further aid for the Borinage including a loan for an aluminium mill at Ghlin on the understanding that at least one-quarter of its total labour force would be recruited from miners then unemployed and a further loan to build a factory to manufacture rubber goods where 40 per cent of the jobs were intended for discharged miners.[27] In 1970 the Commission supported fifteen investment projects designed to create 11,680 jobs in coal mining regions of which approximately 3,500 were earmarked for workers from the coal and steel industries.[28]

By 1965 the time seemed ripe for a new initiative on redevelopment aid and the decision was taken to enlarge the scope of the programme. A new procedure for application was worked out and the High Authority decided to transfer certain of its reserve monies to redevelopment projects at the expense of its housing programmes so that it would not require to rely solely on funds borrowed at ever increasing rates. Loans were thereafter normally made to cover 30 per cent of the capital expenditure involved, with a higher proportion available in special circumstances. Loans were made for ten to thirteen years, repayable as from the end of the third year and at an interest rate of 4·5 per cent for the first five years rising to 6·5 per cent and normally made in the borrower's national currency.[29] This procedure resulted in an increased number of applications from which the High Authority favoured those able to provide most stimulus, subject to its preference for projects enabling workers to be re-employed in the coal and steel industries or in industries which were major consumers of their products.[30] Although its financial aid was modest in relation to the needs of an area and in comparison with national aid, yet it may have been the final factor in a firm's choice of location. It has thus claimed to be a direct influence on the overall economic structure of a region as well as on the conditions of employment.[31]

With greater experience, redevelopment programmes became more sophisticated and showed more careful timing of re-employment plans, better liaison between old and new employers and a greater awareness of the inter-relationship of projects. Applications for Authority aid were increasingly for schemes which were an integral part of a genuine redevelopment programme rather than isolated requests.[32] Since, however, the Authority's responsibility was linked to the fortunes of the coal and steel industries and it was the Treaty of Rome which bore a mandate for aiding more general area redevelopment, one consequence of this broadening view was to necessitate closer working arrangements between the two Communities in order to concert their help. At the same time, close co-operation with national governments was demanded of the High Authority, which remained as the channel through which requests for help were received and upon whose initiative effective planning depended. Facilities such as the creation of a road infra-structure, telephone supply, the provision of social capital or tax concessions to industry remained the responsibility of national governments, and the capacity of the Authority to supplement cash allowances and retraining schemes or to grant aid projects designed to create employment for workers from Community industries clearly limited its functions to that of supporting activities which could only be carried out by national authorities. Once its role had won acceptance, however, its influence on development was not negligible. Its ability to participate in, or to commission, area studies not only helped to determine the direction in which development should go but enabled it to build up a store of worthwhile expertise, thus increasing the value of its contribution to planning at an early stage. Since it was able to act as the focal point and clearing house for discussion and to maintain contact with official and industrial circles, it was well placed to offer advice and appraisal of development operations and in practice to be associated with all aspects of regional growth rather than solely with the declining fortunes of any one sector of an area's economy.

In order to be effective in encouraging investment the High Authority had to formulate its views on the relative significance of different forms of economic activity for a particular area and to determine the time span over which it as an agency should be concerned. Whilst the setting-up of a new firm might solve the immediate problem of providing alternative employment, it might be one which, on a longer view, did not fit into the economic pattern of an area or which was itself old-fashioned in its products or methods. Thus firms with good prospects and which were well advanced technologically might be more advantageous in the long-run but they might not necessarily be the cheapest to establish or the ones with most jobs to offer. High Authority aid was in practice given to a wide range of new industry although metal working and chemical plants figured largely in its schemes.[33] Step by step, therefore, the Authority was drawn into a position in which the scope of its aid became significantly wider than that originally intended, as the decline of the heavy industrial regions became more marked and regional development grew in importance. Here the work of the High Authority showed its most positive and imaginative side. It was anxious to accept these enhanced opportunities and to associate itself wherever possible with governmental responsibility for the entire process of industrial re-development in an area and to use its initiative to establish a constructive interpretation of the treaty clauses to enable it to do this. Despite its dependence upon the growth of national policies to which it was a supplement and the restrictions inherent in a shortage of funds, the experience was revealing of the potentiality of an international organization to play a positive role in what was becoming a major preoccupation of governments.

II Readaptation Aid

By the late 1950s it had become obvious that there would be periods of very rapid mine closure in the future in which a considerable number of jobs would be lost. Thus during the years 1961 to 1964 there were forty-two closures affecting 6,821 men in Belgium, twenty-four closures involving 4,688 men in Germany and twelve closures affecting 1,155 men in France.[34] It was to deal with this problem that Art. 56 had been reformed in order to make maintenance grants more readily available. As in the case of the transitional convention, the flow of applications made a sluggish beginning and it was not until 1966, with the first request from Luxembourg, that the provisions had been activated for all members. The main beneficiaries were the coal miners and this was noticeably so in Germnay, Belgium and, after 1966, in the Netherlands as the reconstruction drives and phased closures continued.[35] In the period up to September 1960 total disbursement from the High Authority had been 15·7 million units of account, by 1967 the annual budget alone had reached 18·9 million and in 1970 25·2 million units were earmarked for 21,747 workers.[36]

Help from the Community did not usurp the responsibility of either the firm or the national government. Its aid was designed to fit in with the circumstances of the individual case and with national arrangements. Each application had therefore to be considered on its merits and to become the subject of a special agreement between the High Authority and the government concerned. This was, in fact, essential. The scale and intensity of need, local circumstances and national benefits were not uniform. Jobs might be readily available in the district, there might be plans to create them or there might be no alternative to encouraging workers to move. In some cases workers might need to acquire a specialist skill on the basis of their old one, in others to be retrained for quite different work. Some firms could easily reabsorb their workers in another factory or town, others might be able to do so after an extended closure period for modernization, others might be going out of business altogether. Rates and length of unemployment pay also varied, the base of previous earnings used to determine cash payments was not uniform, whilst some countries paid two home allowances for those moving. Nevertheless, a general outline within which individual agreements fell is discernible and there appeared some tendency for forms of assistance and the degree of protection offered to become standardized.[37] Agreements between the High Authority and governments normally followed a similar pattern. Where a worker had a temporary period of unemployment to be bridged but expected to go back to his old job, he received an allowance for a twelve to fifteen month period (such allowances were paid for a two-year period to some miners in the Centre-Midi coal fields) either at his full wage or a substantial percentage of it. Similar arrangements applied if he accepted occupational training for a new job[38] which might attract further benefits such as a bonus for successful completion of the course. A new job at a lower wage attracted a benefit to make the worker's total income up to 90 to 100 per cent[39] of his previous earnings for a similar period.[40] Sometimes a lump sum was paid instead of a temporary allowance in order to enable a worker to set up as self-employed. If he sought a job in a new area he was entitled to a lump-sum resettlement allowance varying according to the size of his family and also to removal expenses. In Germany, the Netherlands (and Lorraine) he obtained a special travelling allowance if he did not move home but had to travel a considerable distance to his new place of work or to maintain two homes. If he remained unemployed he received an allowance for a twelve to fifteen month period which normally progressively declined from the full wage to perhaps 60 per cent of it.[41] In 1968 the general principle of a lump-sum payment was established for certain categories. Those over forty years of age with a minimum of five years' service or physically handicapped and taking new posts outside the industries altogether or training courses for this purpose, those still unemployed when the tide-over allowances ended and those elderly or handicapped workers with thirty years' continuous service were all eligible for such payments to which the Commission agreed to contribute a maximum of 625 units of account.[42]

Most redundant workers found new work quickly, but only in Germany were significant numbers of miners able to find fresh jobs in the mines.[43] Whilst, however, alternative employment opportunities were to be found in the buoyant industrial regions in the Ruhr, elsewhere they could remain very limited. In areas where coal had been the predominant industry for many years, such as the Borinage, or where a coal field had been exploited in the middle of a rural area, as in the centre of France, no fresh jobs were to be found and more radical measures to create new employment or to help men to move were necessary. It was clear, too, that the re-employment of the elderly or the physically handicapped miner presented difficulties to which no one found a satisfactory solution. In some schemes he received preferential allowances [44] in recognition of the fact that he was in practice experiencing premature retirement.[45] This was of particular concern in Belgium because of the severe curtailment of the mining industry. Encouragement to their re-employment was there given through a scheme whereby the High Authority and the Belgian government provided a temporary subsidy for the new employer to help cover wages and social security costs,[46] but the difficulty persisted and 'no method can be regarded as the complete answer to the employment problems of elderly and handicapped workers, but a combination of psychological, legal and financial measures may yield good results'.[47] Finally, schemes were not extended to office or managerial grades who might be in equal need of help when a colliery closed down.

Whilst it is difficult to evaluate the success of these schemes [48] it seems that a high proportion of workers laid off came to benefit from ECSC assistance [49] and the vast majority who were reabsorbed into industry on different jobs found themselves with comparable material standards.[50] National patterns, however, varied considerably. During the years from 1960 to 1964 miners in Germany, and to a lesser extent in Belgium, obtained new employment in other colleries but in France considerable change in the industry of employment occurred. 2,200 workers, mostly French and Belgian, underwent retraining and 3,600 were obliged to move house in order to take up new jobs. The elderly and unfit remained out of work noticeably longer than the average.[51]

These activities of the High Authority suggest that the social purpose of readaptation aid was to maintain the standard of living of the worker at a level comparable to that which he had previously known and to help him continue as an active member of the labour force wherever practicable; 'whilst the threat of unemployment previously placed the worker in a weak position which often limited his freedom, now he is always assured of certain guarantees and he is therefore better able to take decisions and to play an active part in his own readaptation'.[52] Despite the great emphasis laid by the Authority on occupational training, which is discussed in the next chapter, its financial aid was largely directed towards cash benefits rather than to training schemes. Whilst this had the positive advantage that men received benefits more nearly akin to earnings than would have been the case had they had to rely entirely on unemployment benefits, it created the difficulty of preferential treatment for those from ECSC industries in comparison with those laid off from other industries in declining areas. Whilst, for example, a coal miner might receive 80 to 100 per cent of his previous earnings a textile worker might be getting only 30 per cent.[53] There is some evidence that, in consequence, governments were sometimes reluctant to apply for ECSC aid.[54]

The readaptation programme also showed the importance of obtaining close working co-operation between institutions operating at different levels of competence. From the High Authority's point of view, its powers were designed to support, encourage and develop schemes initiated by the members with whom the form and scale of Community help was negotiated in each case. In turn, the state was dependent upon the initiative and understanding of local firms, employment officials and public authorities in asking for the help which would prove the most effective. Detailed liaison at operational level was thus essential at all stages if the assistance given by the High Authority was to be of maximum effectiveness as determined by area development schemes or active techniques for the re-employment of labour. The alternative was for the High Authority to rest content with an interpretation of readaptation limited to the narrower task of maintaining the income of the unemployed. This more positive approach demanded different techniques, above all of a preventive nature, so that plans could be made in advance and unemployment limited if not entirely prevented. The High Authority tried to arrange that retraining, if necessary, should take place before discharge.[55] Constant and intelligent anticipation by employers and governments from whom the first initiative had to come was required, whilst the active co-operation of those on the spot in the operation of a scheme could often mean the re-employment of workers in their old, or nearby, firms. It was, therefore, not possible for the High Authority to be indifferent to what was happening at the level of the firm or pit. Union understanding of the processes involved was known by the High Authority to be important but it was not always achieved.[56] The local employment exchange officials needed information about Community allowances and the willingness to see that men applied for them, as well as a good knowledge of new employment opportunities and the value of retraining courses. Finally, it was important that the psychological climate for both employers and workers was kept buoyant and hopeful so that new jobs were in fact created in mining areas and workers reabsorbed as quickly as possible or helped to move with the minimum of anxiety. The synchronization of old and new employment opportunities was no easy task, and the High Authority encouraged formal agreements between public authorities, firms undergoing conversion and new employers to try to obtain it.[57] In this way, one of the most important questions for European social policy was raised, namely how to integrate the experience, understanding and awareness of need of the local community with the power and resources of a remote administrative machine. Furthermore, the inner dynamic whereby limited social objectives compel any authority towards broader considerations was already to be seen at work. These issues were raised again by the EEC itself.

Table 3.1
Some Examples of Redevelopment Loans Granted in the Period up to 4 July 1967 [58]
(costs in u.a.)

Country	Industry	Total capital cost of project	Loan	New jobs created	Cost per job
Germany	Fibreglass	4·25 m	1·0 m	500	8,500
Belgium	Rubber goods	6·0 m	3·0 m	500	12,000
France	Nuts and bolts	1·9 m	0·56m	148	12,865
	Chemicals	26·0 m	4·0 m	85	305,882
Italy	Thermal power station to rehabilitate Sulcis miners	84·3 m	15·0 m		
Netherlands	Motor cars	80·1 m	9·6 m	6,000	13,351

Table 3.2
Readaptation Assistance under Art. 56 [59]
(m.u.a.)

1960	1961	1962	1963	1964	1965	1966	1967 up to June 30	1970
0·6	3·1	7·0	4·3	2·0	9·3	16·6	12·6	25·2

Table 3.3
Summary of Aid Given by ECSC *under Art. 23 of the Transitional Convention and Art. 56 (2) of the Treaty of Paris by December 1957* [61]
(thousand u.a.)

	Coal Workers	Grants	Iron ore mines Workers	Grants	Steel Workers	Grants	Total Workers	Grants
Germany	171,312	43,812	10,276	1,640	7,775	1,135	189,363	46,587
Belgium	64,004	15,154	37	5	3,649	1,405	67,690	16,564
France	11,266	4,137	7,041	2,351	9,996	2,125	28,273	8,613
Italy	6,391	2,596	1,295	851	17,944	10,231	25,630	13,678
Luxembourg	—	—	220	180	—	—	220	180
Netherlands	22,529	8,419	—	—	—	—	22,529	8,419
Community	275,502	74,118	18,869	5,027	39,334	14,896	333,705	94,041

Table 3.4
Readaptation Aid under Art. 56 by Forms of Assistance as at 31 December 1966 [60]

Assistance	Germany	Belgium (as percentage of total expenditure)	France	Germany	Belgium (number of workers assisted)	France
I Aid to make up redundant workers' incomes						
Tide-over allowance	8·13	26·34	14·99	2,930	?	?
Lump sums	72·45	—	20·45	10,414	—	738
Transitional aid	—	—	306	—		
Re-employment allowance	0·66	60·01a	42·24a	1,188	9,399	3,134a
Compensation for concessionary coal	2·70	For Belg. & Fr. the cost of this item was included in other allowances		Numbers included elsewhere		
TOTAL	84·40	86·35	77·68			
II Aid to help workers take other jobs						
Training overheads	0·17	6·64	14·02	97	776	911
Resettlement costs	7·07	7·01	7·96	1,804	556	1,014
Travel and removal costs	7·86	—	—	10,448	—	—
Separation	0·50	—	0·32	257	—	136
TOTAL	15·6	13·65	22·30			

a includes tiding over allowances paid during attendance at vocational retraining courses

4 Manpower

1 Changes in the Workforce

The severe economic difficulties of the coal industry caused manpower problems of wider ramification than unemployment protection. In 1936 the coal industries of the Community had employed 787,000 workers. In 1950 there were 927,300 men at work [1] but output per man shift had dropped.[2] Until the end of 1957 the overall manpower problem was that of meeting the shortage of labour, particularly of underground workers. Great difficulty was found in maintaining the labour force at about the 1950 figure. 'The outstanding problem in all coalfields remains that of manpower recruitment'.[3] Iron and steel manufacture, and the iron ore mines, were under far less pressure. Shortages were not, of course, uniform over the whole area. Whilst the period from 1950 to 1954 saw a rise in the number employed in all industries in Germany, it saw an overall fall in France and Belgium where the decline in employment in the coal fields was marked.[4] Thus the general buoyancy of demand overlay problems of particular areas, such as the Borinage and Lower Saxony, or of the uneconomic nature of certain iron and steel firms in Italy and France. Within the overall picture of labour shortage it was also possible for employment to fall heavily, and it was here that aid from both governments and High Authority was concentrated.

From 1958, however, the dominating factor was the shrinkage of the needs of the coal industry, although this continued to co-exist with a shortage of labour in particular years or areas. The number employed in the coal industry fell from around 900,000 to 600,000 in the seven years from 1958 to 1965, and in the iron ore mines a labour force of 59,300 contracted to 31,000 between 1957 and 1965.[5] The fall in the number of underground workers was particularly striking. In 1952 683,500 men were working below the surface in the collieries but by 1966 only 358,900 were left.[6] The coal and steel industries nevertheless remained significant employers of labour. In 1966 1·2 million people were working in ECSC industries, of whom 637,400 were in the collieries and 565,000 in the iron and steel industries. By 1970 there were still over one million covered by the Paris Treaty, of whom 437,000 worked in coal, 562,400 in steel and

18,400 in the iron ore mines.[7] Mining in particular had become an un-attractive occupation whose drawbacks were no longer compensated by high wages and an élite status in comparison with other industrial wage earners.

The contraction of the industry led to conditions in which surplus labour in one area existed alongside shortages elsewhere, and the un-certainties of the future encouraged a drift away to other employment, often of those people mining could least afford to lose. It became characterized by high turnover, a heavy reliance upon foreign workers for the less attractive jobs and an ageing labour force, less flexible and less qualified than the new generation to carry the responsibility of modernization. Between 1957 and 1964 some 300,000 miners left their jobs and there was a steady rise in the average age of the working force. In 1957 40·8 per cent of workers in coal and 31·2 per cent of steel workers were under thirty years old. By 1964 these figures had dropped to 28·5 and 26·8 per cent respectively.[8] Consequential difficulties associated with an unstable labour force, such as the provision of training, the ensuring of competent work or finding men suitable for promotion, were experienced even in those areas where demand remained high. Technological changes, too, had important implications for the labour force in that higher skills, better qualifications and a wider range of trades were increasingly sought after.

> The old-style miner is being progressively replaced by a worker assigned to certain more specific tasks. The steel process worker, with skills based mainly on experience, is turning more and more into a machine operator or machine-minder; a new category of technicians is growing up.[9]

As the absolute shortage of labour declined, new emphasis upon the quality of manpower and the stability of its employment became discernible. A high rate of turnover becomes less acceptable when new recruits must be trained and supervised or facilities for retraining and refresher courses provided. A heavy reliance upon foreign workers who do not stay long enough to be a truly economic proposition or even to master the necessary skills but who demand more in the way of training and settlement assistance presents severe problems for the employer. Recruitment of foreign labour, although it varied from year to year, continued to be important in the post-war world and attempts, aided by the ECSC, were made to deal with the industrial, social and family prob-lems that it created. The increasing proportion of jobs which were classified as executive or supervisory [10] also brought with it the need for men who could move on from doing the job to supervising and training others. This again suggested the importance of adequate general educa-tion, as well as the possession of vocation and human skills among the workers who were going to stay long enough in the industry for it to benefit from them.

Although the industries were thus facing a future in which fewer men would be needed, these issues suggested that it would be disastrous to their prosperity if the recruitment of new, young workers were to cease. Yet the young men were no longer automatically following in their father's footsteps down the pits and voluntary departures tended to be more common amongst the younger men. Alternative occupation in building and engineering proved of superior attractiveness so that the coal and steel industries found it necessary to strive for comparable conditions and status. The number of apprentices in the Community industries declined sharply after 1950 and this was due mainly to the severe contraction in the coal industry itself. Yet even here it was necessary to maintain a steady intake of young recruits, although the type of apprenticeship was changing in the direction of training tradesmen such as fitters, mechanics and electricians rather than miners as a general group. Whilst in December 1954 there were 82,000 apprentices in the coal and steel industries, by June 1970 this figure had dropped to 18,800.[11] Apprentices formed 6·6 per cent of the total labour force in coal in 1954 and 2·1 per cent of that in steel; in 1970 they made up 2·4 per cent of the manpower force in coal and 1·5 per cent in iron and steel. The need to ensure the continuance of the supply of apprentices and the relevance of their training for the jobs currently required in the Community industries, more especially coal, meant that one of the first proposals of the High Authority was to organize study sessions in the Ruhr and in Dutch Limburg on the occupational training needs for underground miners and to initiate a study into the methods used in the two areas.[12]

The recruitment and retention of the young, the qualified and the able formed the background to the attempts to make the coal and steel industries more attractive as a career, whilst the search for an effective, stable labour force in mining was one of the impulses leading to the attempts to improve conditions and lay behind the stockpiling programmes, schemes for short-time payments, higher standards of mine safety, effective apprenticeship and in-service training schemes.[13] At the same time the severe and concentrated contraction of employment fell with particular harshness upon the elderly, the immobile and the less well qualified, who were the most likely to suffer loss of employment and be least attractive to new employers. In consequence a policy of easement was required. 'One of the Community's standing major problems is how to adjust its labour force to its production needs while duly observing requirements on the social side'.[14] Early retirement pensions for the elderly, resettlement in areas where mines were still viable and new job creation on the spot were all methods to be tried, and realization of the benefits of providing alternative forms of employment in decaying areas gave an early impetus to regional studies and development plans.[15]

Special problems resulted from the heavy reliance upon foreign labour. Recruitment of non-national personnel into the coal and steel industries of Western Europe, particularly the coal mines, has been traditional. It has not been confined, either in past or present, to labour movements within the boundaries of the Community. Western Germany relied heavily in the early post-war years on recruits from the East; the Hungarian uprising brought in more workers. Turks, Greeks, Spaniards and men from North Africa have all made their contribution to coal production. Throughout the period these men formed an important part of the total working force. In December 1955 12 per cent of those working in coal, 8 per cent of those in the iron and steel industry and over 20 per cent in steel and 10·3 per cent in iron ore. 61,600 men including 13,500 Italians, 12,500 North Africans and 16,100 Turks, were working in coal; 69,100 men, including 23,700 Italians, 10,500 North Africans, 7,900 Turks and 10,200 Spanish and Portuguese were working in steel and 1,900, of whom 1,100 were Italians, were in the iron ore industry,[16] The reliance upon foreign labour varied from country to country. A particularly high proportion of the total labour force in the Belgian coal mines was drawn from beyond the frontier[17] but the French iron and steel industry and iron ore mines also relied heavily on outside help. The vast majority of non-nationals employed in the mines worked underground.

Foreign workers varied, too, in their commitment to work in coal and steel. To many, such employment was the jumping-off ground in so far as national rules allowed them occupational mobility; others were interested in short-term contracts only. The constant turnover in recruitment meant that men left before becoming fully skilled or capable of working complicated machinery. In 1958 42·7 per cent of foreign (excluding frontier) workers in coal and steel had been employed therein for less than five years; 23·1 per cent for five to ten years; 15·2 per cent for ten to fifteen years and 19 per cent for over fifteen years. While 53·4 per cent of Poles had worked for over fifteen years, 58·6 per cent of Algerians had been employed for less than five years.[18]

The consequences of a declining labour force, rapid turnover and the need for new skills involved the High Authority in attempts to increase the attractiveness of working conditions, to aid schemes of occupational training and to safeguard the position of the migrant worker.

II Occupational Training

Given the difficulties of recruitment in the mines and at least a limited
dedication to the free movement of labour, it is perhaps surprising that
little attention was paid in the Treaty of Paris to the question of vocational training. It was, nevertheless, a matter with which the High
Authority was actively concerned.

The coal and steel industries formed a particular example of the
demand for greater technical efficiency. To a shortage of skilled manpower was added the complication of labour surpluses in declining areas.
Humanity, economic pressure and union insistence that there should be
no pit closures without consideration of how to reabsorb the work force
all encouraged policies designed to permit re-employment.[19] In these,
occupational training held an important part as mechanization developed.
Old fashioned 'on-the-job' training methods were less effective than they
once were, since the modern skills demanded more systematic training
courses at varying levels of competence.

> The employment of high efficiency machines capable of performing
> complicated work, and the rapid extension of electrification, are
> resulting in the disappearance of the old-style miner. The all-round
> miner, who used to do all the jobs that had to be done in coal mining,
> is being superseded more and more by workers akin to the usual type
> of regular industrial worker, although they retain certain character-
> istics required specifically for work underground. Similar changes, at
> any rate in certain sections, are taking place in the iron and steel
> industry and the iron-ore mines. . . . The High Authority's conclusion
> is that the employers' and workers' organizations and the enterprises
> must be encouraged to extend the basic and advanced training of
> their personnel at all levels.[20]

The field of vocational training was a particularly attractive one for
the High Authority, in that it could be viewed both as a product of, and
a factor in, the technical progress towards which the treaty was directed.
The High Authority did not, however, receive a direct mandate to develop
training schemes and its activity thus depended upon its determination to
interpret the treaty in such a way that it could carry out work it considered to be of first-class importance. If the general objective of the
treaty and the application of Art. 69 provided the argument for training,
the means was found in the right to call for information in all fields
impinging upon the living and working conditions of the labour force.
Training costs certainly demonstrated the wide variations in employers'
costs of which so much had originally been heard. The 1958 survey of the
High Authority on expenditure by employers on recruitment and
vocational training showed the following variations (see Table 4.1).

Table 4.1

Expenditure on Recruitment and Vocational Training as a Percentage of Employers'
Total Expenditure on Wages and Social Charges [21]

	Coal		Iron and steel		Iron ore	
Highest	Netherlands	3·17	Netherlands	6·45	France	1·91
Lowest	Italy	0·01	Belgium	0·13	Luxembourg	0·06

The interest of the High Authority stretched widely to cover the needs of the apprentice at one end to those of the migrant, the manager and, indeed, the instructor himself at the other. It in no way confined itself to the lower grades of work but its interests went 'right up to the top'.[22] As its experience accumulated, it found its task had become as much that of contact with governments, of concern with the educational systems of the Community and of promotion of co-operation between industry and institutions of technical education as with the activities of industry itself. This it pursued through study conferences and the creation of committees of training specialists 'to enable close contact to be maintained between the industries, the teaching profession and the public authorities'.[23]

The High Authority had no right to *impose* standards of training upon industry. Its position was in consequence dependent upon its ability to persuade governments and firms of the importance of its views, to encourage them to act in conformity with its wishes and to participate in the educational activities of the High Authority which became important and varied. Without constant consultation with governments, employers' and workers' organizations as well as educational establishments the High Authority could neither obtain the necessary information for the formulation of its working nor hope to improve the standards of training provided. Much less could it influence them in a common direction. It had, therefore, a constant programme of committees and study groups, seminars and study visits, publication of reports and the dissemination of information about courses, teaching aids in use and similar topics. Permanent sub-committees on vocational training in both coal and steel brought workers' and employers' organizations together and were used by the High Authority as a means of introducing new ideas. Visits of observation, both within and without the Community, were encouraged. Teams from the coal sub-committee made on-the-spot studies in France and the United Kingdom of the vocational training problems brought by mechanization. In 1960 leading representatives from the German, French and Italian iron and steel industries visited the United Kingdom to study training measures for managerial staff. It was a system which relied upon the exchange of experience and information at both industrial and governmental level as a means of making progress.

Over the years the emphasis in the work done by the High Authority changed. The period from 1953 to 1956 was largely devoted to the initiation and publication of studies showing comparative systems and methods of occupational training; to the training of apprentices, miners and steel workers; to the collection and distribution of teaching material, and to the exchange of experiences in the field of industrial methods. From 1957 onwards a new emphasis was discernible, for the High Authority began to pay more attention to training for teachers, supervisory and middle management posts.[24] In this phase it was concerned to involve governments as well as firms because of its recognition of the need to call upon educational systems for the training of managerial and advisory staff. 'Joint endeavours should be made to work out practical ways and means for ensuring closer and more effective co-operation between the educational authorities and industry'.[25] The third training programme which began in 1961 emphasized this new approach with its stress upon the relation of technical change to labour training needs,[26] the importance of training at higher levels and refresher courses generally to assist the adjustment of training 'to the quickening tempo of technological progress in the coalmining, iron-ore and iron and steel industries'.[27]

One of the effects of the introduction of the ECSC was to stimulate the exchange of information across national frontiers. Very little was known anywhere about training methods in use in other countries, and an early start was made by the High Authority on the publication of a complete monograph on the occupational training for young miners underground, a critical analysis of occupational training facilities in the coal industry and an inventory of teaching aids in use, including films, with the intention of establishing an exchange service for them.[28] It continued to collect information about the training provided and issued a catalogue of training manuals designed to ensure that information could be easily acquired anywhere in the Community about activities in any of its members.[29] It also provided a considerable number of studies of existing training practices, on the changes in job content in the industries as well as on the wider questions of the impact of technological change on manpower needs.[30] The High Authority also worked to stimulate government interest by suggesting to the Council methods whereby both standards or methods might be improved and where international co-operation might prove useful[31] and by holding meetings for government experts. Such a meeting was held in September 1961 at which the High Authority submitted three reports. The first covered the question of co-operation between educational institutions and the coal and steel industries upon which the conference members agreed to act nationally to try to obtain action thereon. Secondly, a report was submitted on the structure and organization of general and technical education in Community countries, and thirdly, a draft of the minimum standards of theoretical knowledge and practical proficiency necessary for the exercise of two basic occupations in the industries was put forward. This last study proved unacceptable to the meeting on the grounds that job content was changing too rapidly for such standards to be practicable. Its aim had been to provide a 'first practical step towards the harmonization of the occupational training of Community workers' and its failure, although minor, was symptomatic of the difficulties of this process.[32]

An important step was taken in 1963 when a group of French iron and steel firms applied for a loan under Art. 54 (2) to cover 40 per cent of the cost of building a training centre and this was followed by a similar request from a German steel firm under Art. 54 (1). Both applications were accepted [33] and marked a new departure in the range of the High Authority's work.

The executives also contributed to the work of training the teachers. Effective vocational training depends to a considerable extent upon their quality, their teaching competence, the up-to-dateness of their technical knowledge and their skill in human relations. A first task, in 1960, was for the High Authority to set up a study group to look at questions of instructor training in the belief that an emphasis upon the quality of the teacher would quickly have repercussions on the level of training as a whole, and to publish the results. It also tried to bring instructors together to help them keep abreast with new development. An example of this was the conference of training officers called in November 1965 on the use of programmed instruction which was becoming more widely used in the coal and steel industries in the course of experimental schemes mounted in collaboration with the High Authority.[34] It also made a contribution through helping to finance meetings of experts and by playing an active part in conferences and study programmes organized by firms.[35]

Today teaching aids take many forms. They can range from standardized manuals of instruction, technical literature, model lessons and programmed learning kits to follow-up studies of the effectiveness of different methods of teaching and to the constant exchange of information. The High Authority collected information about material used in the Community, circularized it, and attempted its standardization and improvement.[36] Its consciousness of the inadequacies of technical training made for an early emphasis on the methods and materials in use and upon trying to fill some of the more obvious gaps. Technical conferences relating to training schemes in both coal and steel were an early achievement; studies made of available teaching aids and reports on the vocational training position in steel were published in 1954.[37] The actual exchange of teaching material, so important for the improvement and alignment of standards, nevertheless proved difficult because of the reluctance of national governments to remove the customs duties impeding it. In consequence the High Authority requested governments to set up an expert working party to consider the removal of these barriers by studying the exact nature of the legal and administrative regulations involved with a view to allowing temporary duty free entry.[38] By 1959 the High Authority had a draft of the laws which operated to prevent the exchange of teaching aids for submission to government experts for their examination with a view to abolition or simplification. The working party ultimately put forward a number of suggestions [39] which the High Authority attempted to put into practice. Delays continued, however, until 1964. It then became possible, under Art. 155 of the Rome Treaty, to formulate a recommendation to governments asking for the elimination of administrative and customs formalities impeding the exchange of teaching aids by allowing their temporary import for educational or training purposes to be free of duty and taxes.[40]

The work of the High Authority had two related, but distinct, objectives. The first was to improve the standard of instruction through the provision of practical assistance with the difficulties encountered by firms at all levels of their training programmes. Its studies of vocational training issues, its proposals to members on ways of improving vocational training and its grant aid for centres, study visits and conferences were directly designed to do this and should have helped to establish a favourable climate of opinion towards the need for occupational training. The second was to encourage the alignment of standards as a contribution towards the objectives of free movement and the harmonization of working conditions. Here its contribution was less positive, and no definite results can be attributed to the work of the High Authority in this connection.

The necessity to rely upon migrant workers was widely accepted during the labour shortages of the 1950s but their high turnover, language limitations and lack of qualifications often made their employment of doubtful value. On the whole, it was the unskilled who were ready to seek employment elsewhere, yet their training was often an uneconomic proposition for individual firms, needing special attention to be effective. This seemed an issue particularly suitable for action at an international level and in 1957 it was agreed that the High Authority should investigate the best methods of migrant training. At that time it was hoped to set up pilot centres both in the country of origin to provide general induction services, language and industrial safety tuition as well as in the receiving country where more intensified vocational training might be given,[41] but the falling-off in recruitment of migrant labour which followed meant that these projects were not further developed. Neither did the High Authority do much to formalize minimum standards of proficiency although it 'has been recognized that there must be progressive harmonization of the knowledge and abilities of the workers engaged on skilled trades: this is one of the fundamental prerequisites to any true common market for labour'.[42] Since a free labour market within the Community was only demanded for workers of definite qualifications, the promotion of training courses might have served this purpose as well as easing the difficulty of recruiting men of adequate calibre. Underlying this question, however, was the problem of the recognition of training and qualifications, and it was therefore in the interest of the High Authority at the very least to encourage understanding of, and interest in, the training systems in use within members and the standards set for qualifications obtained. In consequence, issues of educational levels at entry into training courses, scholastic content and the grading of skills came to be ones of international importance. The ideal solution of uniformity of standards and corresponding adjustment of course content remained a long-term objective of the High Authority. The 'overall aim is to harmonize the objectives of initial, follow-up and advanced training and standardize qualifications' [43] but its later reports expressed little optimism about the possibility of overcoming the obvious difficulties in the way of harmonization.

> While fully recognizing that the methods and content of occupational training must be adapted to the different parts of the Community, the High Authority is endeavouring, with an eye to ultimate harmonization, to find a Community-level solution to the regularly recurring problems facing those concerned with personnel training.[44]

This cautious approach was dictated both by its lack of direct legal powers and by its recognition that the imposition of common standards was hampered by ingrained difficulties between members concerning work and training practices.[45] National arrangements for industrial training which had grown up over the years and represented a complex of educational forces, traditional customs, restrictive practices and industrial attitudes could not be dismantled overnight. It was at times found easier to work for comparability of standards in the new jobs that were being demanded by modern industry than to do battle in more traditional fields of job organization.

Under such circumstances, its success in both aims was dependent on co-operation with interested parties, the constant interchange of experience and the dissemination of suggestions designed to stimulate government departments and employers to initiate or step up training measures.[46] If uniformity of standards was too advanced an aim, measures to increase understanding of the training systems in use within the members and of the standards used in establishing qualifications were at least a step in the right direction. Here, too, lay the importance of all co-operative ventures at Community level, of work designed to formulate standards of job content, qualification and training to be utilized through the Community area and the use of training manuals which it was hoped would come to be generally used. Such activity was basically an educational one which demanded skills of persuasion and argument to be devoted to overcoming outmoded views on industrial training, national prejudices and protective procedures and to obtaining acceptance of the notion of the role of the High Authority. Its work was inevitably in part a pioneering venture to establish the justification for an international interest in industrial training schemes designed to lead to international standards.

III The Free Movement of Labour

Although the coal and steel industries relied heavily on foreign labour, excluding frontier workers, free access to jobs did not exist at the time of the creation of the common market. Controls over movement had been heavily increased during the war and, despite attempts at liberalization under the auspices of OEEC, members were not ready to abandon them in 1951 at a time when fears of the influx of cheap labour remained high. Employers, therefore, relied on recruiting programmes and any socially supportive services were normally provided by them. Such services customarily included basic travel arrangements, induction procedures and hostel accommodation.

From a social point of view, the Treaty of Paris was imperfectly designed. The industries were heavily dependent upon foreign labour, notably to perform the lowest tasks, but the treaty was confined to the movement of skilled labour and to the possibility of the reabsorption of existing coal and steel workers elsewhere in the Community.[47] At the same time safeguards against the influx of cheap labour were written into the treaty both by forbidding the cutting of wages as a competitive tool and the refusal to allow discrimination in pay between nationals and non-nationals. These arrangements hardly amounted to acceptance of the principle of free movement as a basic norm of social policy although some movement of workers away from areas of poor conditions into more favourable ones was expected to play a part in the pursuit of the long-term goal of the equalization of conditions of life and work.[48]

> Nevertheless it is to be expected that the fact that *workers will have the right to go to areas where wages and living conditions are more favourable will increasingly exert a pressure to raise wages* in the coal and steel industries where they are the lowest and that technically qualified workers, in particular, will be encouraged to migrate.[49]

The development under the Treaty of Paris towards expression of the notion of a 'common professional nationality'[50] carrying with it the right of the individual to select his place of work[51] was more important as a first step towards acceptance of such a social principle and as a guide to its implementation. This is particularly so since there was in practice little migration of skilled workers, to whom the principle applied, for they were in great demand everywhere and had little incentive to overcome the difficulties attendant on moving to a new country. Where national frontiers cut across industrial complexes the same difficulties did not, of course, apply.[52] Similarly, the Coal and Steel Community provided a useful experience in dealing with the human aspects of migration through consideration of those factors, whether social, economic or administrative in nature, which hampered the recruitment of labour.

Practical steps to ensure the free movement of skilled workers were left for future negotiation between members. The function of the High Authority under Art. 69 was limited to 'guide and facilitate the implementation by Member States of the measures provided'. Its first step was to set up a working party, which began work in March 1952,[53] to discuss the definition of jobs, the level of qualification to be considered as appropriate for different grades, the length of time which should have been worked in the industry or in the job in question and the extent to which a job performed in the coal and steel industry should be distinguished from the identical one performed elsewhere. It was not the High Authority's view that workers who had been employed in coal and steel for only a few weeks should automatically become eligible for the benefits of Art. 69, but that a period such as two years' work in coal and three in steel was necessary.[54] Where a job was specific to the industry, the problem was one of determining the level of qualifications, including if appropriate a minimum working period, necessary for eligibility. Further problems concerned the nature of the limitation which might be exercised for the protection of public order and health, the elaboration of methods to co-ordinate offers of work with existing vacancies and the way to improve the social security position of migrants. The High Authority submitted its general views on the importance of these matters and the need to consider them further to the Council on 16 December 1953,[55] whilst pointing out that other requirements of the treaty, namely the prevention of discrimination between national and other workers over pay and conditions of work and the amendment of immigration laws in order to permit the re-employment of coal and steel workers from elsewhere within the Community, were largely matters of internal administration for which members would have to act directly themselves.

As a result of this preliminary discussion, an inter-governmental conference on the movement of labour met on 15 May 1954, which agreed on certain cautious moves. A degree of relaxation of migration control was established for qualified workers, although these were still to be defined in stringent fashion, by the creation of a system to allow eligible workers to accept jobs offered to them although not to seek work actively. Arrangements were put in hand for a further conference designed to achieve a European convention on the social security of migrants and the High Authority and the ILO began preliminary work on this in the summer. Specific proposals on labour movement were formally accepted by the Council on 8 December 1954 which then required ratification by government with appropriate amendments to municipal legislation. Under the arrangements,[56] qualified personnel eligible for the application of the principle of free movement were defined on the basis of two criteria relating respectively to job definition and the length of time worked therein. Fifty-six jobs were specified: twenty-nine in coal and twenty-seven in steel. They were not limited to trades but included foremen, managerial and supervisory posts. Those qualified by systematic training required one year's work during the preceding three years; those qualified only by practical training required two years' work in a Community industry and one year's work (which could be part of the two-year stint) on the job in question. The two years had to have been worked in the previous three. In either case the worker had to have been paid a rate above the unskilled rate. Such workers became eligible for a 'European labour card' obtainable from their regional labour exchange allowing them to take work in the specific category for which they were qualified without having to obtain a labour permit under national legislation. They were therefore free to respond to an offer of suitable employment anywhere in the Community whether this came directly from an employer in writing or through an official labour exchange as part of a recruitment scheme. Although only valid for a particular type of job it was understood that a state might permit a card holder to move into other work.[57] Administrative requirements, covering matters such as the issue and renewal of cards, for two years in the first instance, the notification of jobs and available workers, and co-ordination between employment exchanges to determine the type of information required, were approved by the Council in July 1955 but slow ratification of the rules by Germany and Luxembourg[58] meant a delay in operating them until 10 September 1957. Community supervision was exercised through a Technical Commission chaired by M. Mansholt, then Permanent Under-Secretary of the Dutch Ministry of Social Affairs, manned by official experts in labour placing services, whilst the High Authority provided the secretariat.

The decision of December 1954 envisaged the possibility of extension in the list of skilled occupations approved for the purposes of Art. 69 through the submission of a proposal from the High Authority and two member governments to the Council. On 15 October 1959, member states set up a directing committee to arrange for a further inter-governmental meeting the following autumn to agree upon those jobs which would in future be eligible for the European labour card. On 16

May 1961 the Council duly adopted the amendments[59] and by the middle of 1963 all governments had informed the Council's Secretariat that municipal legislation had received the necessary alterations and the new list became operative from July.[60] It contained a further 118 jobs: eighty-seven in iron and steel and thirty-one in the coal mines, and included occupations not peculiar to the coal and steel industries provided they were exercised in a special way. 'The only occupations excluded are unskilled jobs requiring no training or initiation.'[61] Later in the year the position of migrants in those industries was further affected by the entry into force of EEC Regulation 15 which began the institution of free movement of labour for the economy as a whole. It was specifically laid down that nothing in the regulation should be used to detract from the provisions under the Treaty of Paris or the rights of the possessors of the European labour card, but where workers in coal and steel were not covered by special arrangements then the provisions of Regulation 15 were to apply. The most important aspect of this arrangement for workers in coal and steel concerned the admission to, and employment in, the host community of family workers and the possibility for workers to move out of the industries into other jobs after a specific period.

Although it was claimed that three to four hundred thousand workers could be affected by the arrangements,[62] the number taking advantage of them proved to be very small. During the first year of work only 283 cards were issued; Italy received 124, Belgium 94, Germany 57 and the Netherlands obtained 8. Two hundred and forty-eight cards were for jobs in the coal and iron ore mines.[63] By 30 September 1965 only a total of 1,806 cards had been provided.[64] Furthermore the number of jobs which in reality benefited from the scheme was in fact far smaller since some cards were issued to men already working in skilled jobs in a country other than their own, but it must also be remembered that considerable movement between the Benelux countries or across frontiers occurred without the aid of these special facilities and that bilateral recruiting schemes often acted as an alternative method of obtaining available skilled men. Nevertheless the paucity of such labour meant that attention had perforce to be paid to the effective use of unskilled, foreign labour often drawn from agricultural areas such as the south of Italy which provided a steady stream of workers, particularly for the coal mines of Belgium. During 1956 the High Authority began discussion with employers' and workers' organizations concerning recruitment problems, particularly in Germany and France, in order to try to encourage proper attention to the attendant problems. It also approached governments to discover what steps had been taken by them to revise their immigration laws in order to relieve the labour shortage and to facilitate the re-employment of skilled workers under Art. 69 (3). The previous year it had commissioned a study of the obstacles to the free movement of labour showing the complexity of the phenomenon, the variety of migratory movements and the importance of a wide range of facilities and services if mobility was to be effective both economically and socially.[65] The report brought out in particular the marginal value of migration to skilled men unless substantial inducements were involved, its greater attraction to the young and relatively rootless, the importance of housing facilities as a draw for incoming labour, the often inadequate vocational training assistance provided for migrants, the value of good public relations, welfare facilities and careful preparation for the move. It thus emphasized the need for care over selection, recruitment and initiation into work, the systematic consideration of family settlement and adequate housing, and the need for attention to integration both on and off the job whether the migrants were Community nationals or not.

By 1965 the High Authority had a number of studies and surveys either completed, or under way, as a guide to measures for better recruitment and the safer and more productive employment of foreigners as means of reducing the instability of the labour force. On the grounds that foreign workers might well become an increasing proportion of the whole, the High Authority began to pay more systematic attention to their needs. It began a special study of the adaptation problems of migrants, the various selection and recruitment procedures in use, the entry and residence conditions for foreign workers and their families, their reception and employment arrangements and housing.

Whilst foreign labour recruitment was little influenced numerically by the existence of the ECSC, the positive side of the Treaty of Paris was the concept of the international labour market for the skilled worker and the encouragement to member states to ease entry in order to relieve the manpower shortage. The economic pressures resulting from the conditions operative in the coal and steel industries and the high demand for skilled labour everywhere were far more important in determining human movements, so that the role of the High Authority remained a limited one increasingly overshadowed by the wider responsibilities of the EEC deriving from the principle of the free movement of labour for all workers.

It has long been recognized that the development of social security schemes necessitates that the needs of the migrant worker be given special consideration. The growth of such protection, and particularly of social insurance arrangements, meant that he would be penalized if treaty arrangements were not made to allow for the export of earned benefits and, where necessary, for the exclusion of migrants from nationality and residence rules. This type of international co-operation is of longstanding in Western Europe stretching back to the Franco–Italian labour treaty of 1904. After the Second World War a

number of moves were made to make protection more effective and to
lift it out of bilateral treaty arrangements by the adoption of more
general principles to which a number of states might adhere, thus introducing more flexibility which was of particular help to those who spent
their working lives in two or more countries. In particular, the Nordic
Council, Western European Union, Benelux, the Council of Europe and
the European Communities developed multilateral systems through which
entitlement earned before migration could be recognized subsequently
and benefits paid to workers wherever they might be within the
appropriate region.

The Treaty of Paris accepted the general principle of non-discrimin-
ation between national and migrant workers placing special emphasis
upon the need to prevent social security systems operating as an obstacle
to labour mobility. It gave to the High Authority the responsibility of
guiding state action in this field. The matter proved an extremely complex
one, not only because of the existence of many bilateral arrangements
and the wish to see them merge into wider systems but because of the
difficulty of dealing with social security problems in the coal and steel
industries without considering them for workers generally. The work
done by the High Authority was, therefore, only a preliminary to that
accomplished by the European Economic Community, and the discussion of the resolution of the issue is postponed until Volume 2. However,
as a result of discussions between the High Authority and the ILO, a
conference of experts met in Geneva in July 1954 to consider not merely
the position of the many non-nationals working in the coal and steel
industries but an ILO draft for a multilateral convention to cover migrants
generally which might serve as the basis for wider European agreement
on the subject. Three years later, on 9 December 1957, the European
Convention on Social Security for Migrant Workers was signed by the
Ministers of Labour of the six members meeting in Rome. The document,
which was intended to be available for others to sign, was designed to co-
ordinate national social security schemes and to ensure that migrants
would not lose their benefits by providing for the addition of periods of
employment in order to establish eligibility and the amounts of benefit
payable and to arrange for the provision of benefits, both in cash and in
kind, where a worker or his family was outside the country of employment. The convention applied to wage-earners, with certain definite exceptions, and covered the main branches of social security, namely sickness
and disability benefits, old age pensions, payments to dependants, insurance against industrial accidents and diseases, family allowances and
unemployment pay. It superseded bilateral and multilateral conventions
which up till then had governed social security for migrants retaining
some exceptions for special cases and for frontier workers.[66] The implementation of the convention was put in the hands of an Administrative

Commission to represent the signatories, the High Authority and the ILO. Its responsibility was to see that the convention was identically interpreted, to settle difficulties of interpretation, to promote closer co-operation on health and social matters and to be responsible for the arrangements as between such countries as wished to use it for settling claims arising out of the payment of benefits under the convention. This document was ultimately converted into Regulations 3 and 4 of the EEC but migrants from outside the Community still depended upon special bilateral agreements, modified if both parties accepted ILO or Council of Europe standards, and the High Authority retained a special responsibility for examining their problems since many of them were drawn to the coal and steel industries.

5 The Improvement of Living and Working Conditions

I Introduction

With the creation of the ECSC, the High Authority found itself with the general responsibility to promote better living and working conditions in such a way as to permit their equalization but with no precise direction as to how this could, or should, be done. It was not clear what effect the new framework for the industries would have upon the conduct of industrial relations or what relationship would develop between the High Authority and collective bargaining procedures. However, the establishment of good working patterns between the High Authority, employer and worker organizations was a necessary precondition of the executive's work in order to obtain adequate information to establish policies and to ensure their prosecution at industrial or political level. It has already been seen that the Treaty of Paris itself recognized the necessity to associate employers' organizations and unions with its operation, but a new question was of the extent to which claims would henceforth be presented at European level. The Joint Committees on the Harmonization of the Terms of Employment in Steel and Coal respectively, which were formally constituted by 1958,[1] provided a new forum for the discussion of employment problems. Even during periods of difficulty on the coal committee, when it was boycotted by the miners' unions, working parties on questions such as hours of work and industrial relations continued to meet.[2] Such committees enabled the High Authority to make contact with experts on both sides of industry for its studies and investigations and thus played a part in exposing the differences which existed between one country and another concerning working conditions.

A first question for the High Authority was the definition of its task. In February 1954 it asked the consultative committee to study the problem of the appropriate action to be undertaken for the harmonization of conditions. In its reply the committee argued that there would be a need to call meetings of a tripartite character to study the problems associated with such a policy, that it would be wise to consider the easiest problems first, namely questions such as the regulation of the hours of work, the payment of fringe benefits, rates for night work, Sundays and public holidays, the length of holidays and payment for them. Finally, it suggested that the High Authority itself should both make a study of the existing situation and the problems it saw and consider the various means available by which modifications in current practices might be achieved in order to make harmonization a reality.[3]

This resolution led the Authority to determine that its policy would be to assemble and study the necessary documentary material which it could then pass on to employers' and workers' organizations for them in turn to consider if any points could, or should, be incorporated in collective bargaining agreements. The Assembly reinforced this view in May 1955, requesting the High Authority and governments to collaborate with the two sides of industry in ways of working towards the harmonization of existing regulations concerning working conditions, especially the number of hours worked, overtime benefits, holidays allowed and the rates of holiday pay.[4]

Meanwhile the Authority began an active study programme working through its joint committee structure or through sponsoring agency studies. These ranged over topics such as wage levels, social security benefits, the nature of the labour contract, the impact of technological change on productivity, the length of the working day, the reasons for miners leaving their jobs and why young people took other employment.[6] A great deal of this work was continuous, but a first priority was to establish the factual situation in the members as a basis for any subsequent action devoted to harmonization. Memoranda on legal provisions in each member were drawn up covering collective bargaining systems and other methods, if any, of regulating conditions of employment, as well as the regulations concerning working hours, their definition and exceptions allowed to the regulations, rules and pay for Sunday and holiday work and holidays with pay.[6]

The consultative committee, however, was anxious to see discussions on the expert committees progress from checking the accuracy of the facts to debating the conclusions that should be drawn from them in order to harmonize conditions of employment,[7] thereby establishing the right of debate and concern at Community level. The problem was well illustrated by the attempt to use the joint coal committee as a forum for the discussion of a miners' charter as a first step towards the harmonization of standards in the mines.

During 1956 the problem of recruitment to the coal mines was particularly severe and considerable attention was given by the High Authority to a number of matters likely to affect recruitment favourably. Its interest was sparked off by the action of the German government in paying a tax-free shift bonus.[8] Although the original method of payment was considered by the High Authority to be incompatible with the treaty,[9] it was nevertheless far from disapproving of the idea of a bonus as a means of attracting extra workers. The idea rapidly developed to include the demand for better overall conditions in the coal industry and was supported by the unions in an attempt to achieve an interpretation of the treaty commitment as one requiring the establishment of high, uniform standards throughout the Community area. The High Authority prepared draft proposals to include better pensions, a guaranteed wage and greater regularity of employment, better vocational training, housing conditions, transport between home and work, seniority and long-service bonuses.[10] These formed the basis of the European miners' charter and became the subject of very considerable discussion. The attraction of such a programme to the High Authority was obvious, not only as a means of dealing with immediate manpower difficulties but as a bid for the improved and harmonized living and working conditions to which the treaty was committed. It thus formed one part of the attempt to establish a Community framework for the coal industry. On the one side was a Community energy policy within which coal would take its place and the industry be supported on the basis of rules determined at Community level, and on the other a social programme for the workers for 'there will be no more miners unless a bold social policy is adopted'.[11]

The matter was examined exhaustively by both the ICFTU and the Christian Trade Unions as well as by the Social Affairs Committee of the European Parliament. The Parliamentary Resolution on the social problems of coal[12] drew attention to the difficulties of the mining industry and the need to safeguard the employment and the social position of the miners. It also stressed the need to maintain a core of effective workers and was anxious to see the High Authority collaborate with employers' and workers' organizations in a general policy of a five-day and forty-hour week with no loss of pay. It argued that new employment outlets and readaptation measures should be put into operation in areas where mine closures were occurring; that the High Authority should collaborate with governments and industry on long-term readaptation programmes by which the dislocation resulting from mine closures might be minimized. In the meantime the miners should receive payment for lost wages. It recommended that the High Authority should watch to see if resources made available for readaptation were enough and work closely with the European Investment Bank, the social fund and the Commission. Finally, the High Authority should take urgent steps to elaborate the miners' charter.

Labour organizations within the Community had for some years been concerned with the need for more stability and regularity of employment and had been working nationally on issues such as a guaranteed income, security of employment and the certainty of an old age pension.[13] The generalization of such demands was to their obvious advantage. Within the official structure of the Community, however, the matter made little progress.[14] No effective forum for the discussion of the proposed charter existed, since the attempts of the High Authority to create a joint organization of employers and workers were themselves foundering on the issue of government representation.[15] As a result, the tripartite Joint Committee on the Harmonization of Terms of Employment in the Coal Mining Industry, under the chairmanship of the High Authority, which had been set up in 1954, waited four years until its first meeting in June 1958. On 17 October the workers' representatives asked for a study of the charter to be made but the employer members of the committee argued that they were not authorized so to do, and since two and a half years elapsed before the next meeting of the committee it was not until 15 December 1961 that the workers' representatives were able to ask formally for a discussion of the suggested code. This was again postponed at the request of the employers, and the High Authority agreed to send out factual material on the position in the member countries. It was also suggested at the meeting that the employers' associations should empower their representatives to discuss the subject at the next meeting scheduled for 6 July 1962. This discussion duly took place, but no action could be agreed upon although the union members spoke strongly in its favour both as a means of harmonization of conditions and as an antidote to the high turnover of labour: 'The Government and employers' representatives, however, opposed almost to a man the whole principle of a European Miners' Code',[16] believing that a first priority towards social progress was the improvement of economic conditions and the adoption of a definite energy policy within which a social policy for the miners could be evolved. The Italian and Belgian government representatives proved the only ones in favour. The German official attitude was that the labour contract was autonomous and that the Community had no competence in the matter; the latter argument was supported by the French government representatives whilst the Dutch member argued it was inopportune to discuss the matter. The German employers argued the High Authority had no rights in the affair since the issues were ones properly to be settled by social legislation or by the two sides of industry themselves, whilst the French, Belgian and Dutch employers stressed the high social charges which would result for the employers from the adoption of the charter. Only the Italian employers' representatives felt the matter might be discussed.[17] Other ideas were put forward at the meeting as being possibly more helpful than the code itself. These included the generalization of the German shift bonus, the scaling-down of the social charges of the collieries and a drive to restore confidence in European coal. The High Authority's suggestion of a working party to study the draft code and estimate its cost was, however, unacceptable to both the employers' and government representatives.

On 25 September the High Authority reported to the Social Affairs

Committee in the following terms. The treaty did not compel the two sides of industry and governments to participate in discussion designed to have a concrete result in social matters, neither was the High Authority given the general power to issue proposals, opinions and recommendations which could only be done in those cases explicitly provided for in the treaty. It was, therefore, entirely for the parties to decide in this particular case if the talks should continue and what, if anything, should be done to give effect to the code. Nevertheless, the High Authority argued that it had been right to place the item on the agenda at the request of one of the members, and right to assist in the discussion by producing an explanatory memorandum, in proposing the establishment of a working party and in placing the necessary material and facilities at the disposal of both employers and workers. The High Authority therefore continued with its efforts to bring both sides of industry together in the ensuing weeks and stood by its proposal for a working party, for 'the High Authority feels that, in the interest both of the men and of the collieries themselves, action will have to be taken in the matter of the Code'.[18] The initiatives taken by the High Authority were supported by the Social Affairs Committee on the grounds that they were a means of maintaining a more stable labour force and adequate recruitment and as matters which fell within the competence of the High Authority.[19]

Nevertheless, the matter remained deadlocked. The High Authority met privately with representatives of workers, employers and governments to attempt to find a basis for opening formal discussion, but it was still only the workers' representatives who were in favour of exploring the issue in some form of mixed commission. It produced a memorandum for Parliament on the progress of the negotiations[20] and President Del Bo addressed Parliament on 26 November on the matter.

No agreement was reached in 1963 on discussion within the joint committee, but the following year saw more dramatic developments. A meeting of the committee was held on 24 April 1964 to discuss social security arrangements at which the representatives of the ICFTU asked for the question of the miners' charter to be placed on the agenda. When this was refused by both government and employer members, the ICFTU delegates left the meeting which came to an end at that point. Private discussions were thereupon resumed throughout the year by the High Authority with the parties but no plenary sessions of the committee were held since the ICFTU delegates refused to attend unless the charter was discussed.

In the summer a rally of twenty thousand miners drawn from seven unions within the Community affiliated to the ICFTU was held at Dortmund to demonstrate the solidarity of the workers behind a European movement incorporating social ideals and in particular to support the project for a European miners' code. President Del Bo addressed the meeting at length on the subject of the proposed charter recalling that M. Finet, as long ago as 1956, had foreshadowed the emergence of such a charter ensuring certain benefits to all miners, irrespective of origin or nationality. He argued that, since the adoption of the energy protocol in April 1964, there was now no logical reason for refusing discussion on the charter itself which was designed to provide a career structure, better accident services and other necessary advantages. The cost would be considerable and this would have to be faced. The meeting passed three major resolutions demanding an effective common energy policy, intensification of the work of the High Authority in a wide range of social matters and deploring the non-adoption of the miners' charter. The meeting showed clearly the inter-relationship of a possible energy policy, a more clearly defined role for coal and the social developments for which a call was being made. It openly expressed its dissatisfaction with the lack of progress made over the charter since it was first mooted in October 1957.[21]

On 26 October 1964 M. Finet spoke in Parliament stressing the importance of the charter as a means of recruitment of new miners and the determination of the High Authority to promote new contacts between the three protagonists. He suggested that the application of the Protocol of Agreement on an Energy Policy might provide the opportunity for a step forward. On 18 December all the workers' representatives on the committee agreed to meet with the High Authority. Whilst strong support of the charter was maintained, both ICFTU and IFCTU members proved themselves willing to see it introduced in stages. In order to make an immediate appeal to new recruits, they considered that the first step should be the general introduction of the German shift bonus and a loyal service payment. The former would constitute official recognition of the hard and dangerous life of the underground worker 'and would be a first step towards exempting Community miners' wages from taxation';[22] the latter would be an encouragement to more stable employment. The workers' representatives argued the case for the changes in terms of the need to improve the status of mining to attract and maintain an effective labour force which would itself improve the working conditions of the industry because it would be more efficient, more capable of handling complex machinery, improving safety standards and benefiting from further training. Nevertheless, their agreement to concentrate upon two specific items rather than the whole programme represented a significant shift in policy.

Th proposals were put to employers and government representatives in the New Year. The employers' meeting of 19 February 1965 was boycotted by the French, who argued such matters could only be considered by the French government, and by the Dutch, who claimed they had not had sufficient time to consult amongst themselves. The German and Belgian delegates declared that, whilst they were not against the internationalization of the shift bonus, further clarification was required as to its implications and on whether all employers' federations and governments would agree to it. A few days later the government representatives of the five coal producing countries met, but strong differences of view were expressed. Some members believed that neither the High Authority, nor the joint committee, had any jurisdiction in matters connected with wage payments and only the Council, representing the members, had the right to discuss this. The meeting did, however, agree that the High Authority should compile a full record of both types of bonus already being used within the Community and this information was presented to a meeting of the joint committee itself on 24 June. It was agreed that discussion of the arrangements should be continued at a further meeting.

Meanwhile, the previous February, both the ICFTU and the IFCTU had sent their official proposals to the High Authority. These asked that both types of bonus should be incorporated in a new form of 'ECSC allowance'. The concept was included by the High Authority in its recommendations contained in its Memorandum on Coal Policy up to 1970 submitted to the Council in March along with the Authority's own suggestions intended to enable the coal industry to retain the services of an adequate number of skilled young workers. An *ad hoc* committee was set up to study the bonus question and by this procedure it moved away from the joint committee to become a Council matter. Meanwhile, the adoption of the miners' charter itself remained as far off as ever.

The episode showed clearly the limitations on the capacity of the High Authority to influence social conditions directly despite strong support from Parliament and the trade unions or even to get a joint discussion going. From the point of view of harmonization of working conditions, the problem of whether union demands would in future always be pitched at the level of the highest national arrangement in every particular underlay the debate. Additionally France, whose mines were nationalized, feared to set off a chain reaction of workers' claims within the public industries as a whole. Improved conditions in the mines were thus the subject of national measures during these years, for attractions there had to be in order to deal with recruitment difficulties.

II Investigations into Wages and Working Conditions

The establishment of the Coal and Steel Community meant the possibility to begin to collect information in standardized form; to make comparisons, to study trends and generally to provide information which might be used at national level for bargaining purposes.[23] The first studies of wages had perforce to concern themselves with definition and the problems involved in the collection of data in comparable form. Two expert tripartite committees were set up to establish a nomenclature of all elements making up wages, but ran into considerable technical difficulties over terminology and different national methods of data collection[24] so that the statistical basis of the work produced in the early years was recognized as being far from perfect. Despite this, two outstanding conclusions emerged from the early studies. The first published material showed the importance of social charges other than wages in total labour cost, whilst later work demonstrated the tendency for that social element to increase more rapidly than the strict financial return.[25] The second early study of great interest was that published on real incomes received within the coal and steel industries suggesting that differences in real incomes were not as great as popularly supposed and certainly no greater than those found within members between different regions or industries.[26] Italy formed the only serious exception.

By 1958 the High Authority was in a position to publish information concerning wage trends in Community industries showing rates of increase in coal and steel of comparable magnitude but in each case increases in the Netherlands were particularly high.[27] The relative order of labour costs in the coal mines remained very similar for the first years of the common market in which the Saar and France were the top rankers, Italy at the bottom with the remainder jostling for the middle places.[28] However, the rate of increase of total wage costs between 1952 and 1958 was greater in the countries where labour costs were least.

Consideration of the total wage costs in the steel industry showed a similar, though less clear, conclusion that the ranking order of countries remained the same during the six years (see Table 5.1). Luxembourg remained at the top with either the Saar or Belgium in second place, France and Germany competing for third place and Italy and the

Table 5.1
Total Wage Costs in the Steel Industry, 1952 and 1958[29]
(Belgian francs)

	Luxembourg	Saar	Belgium	France	Germany	Italy	Netherlands
1952	48·96	37·33	41·12	35·69	34·75	31·82	26·45
1958	65·88	55·09	54·61	49·76	52·84	42·97	47·28

Netherlands bringing up the rear in most years. The percentage changes in total wage costs suggested some closing of the gap between the best and worst for it had ranged from 17.8 per cent in 1952 and fallen to 12.7 per cent in 1958.

A later study[30] showed that, excluding Italy, the real income of underground workers in coal moved more closely together during the period from 1954 to 1958, but that in steel the gaps in real income tended to increase. In the iron ore mines relatively fast increases were made in Germany whilst France caught up with the leader, Luxembourg, so that overall some alignment seemed to have occurred. Workers in 1958 fell into three broad groups. The highest real incomes were received by the iron ore miners of Luxembourg, whilst the French iron ore miner received 90 per cent of the Luxembourg wage and the Luxembourg steel worker 80 per cent. In the middle group came the miners and steel workers of Belgium, the coal miners and steel workers of France and the Saar and the Dutch miners. As a group they earned between 65 and 75 per cent of those at the top in real terms. The poorest paid were the German and Italian workers in all three industries and the Dutch steel workers. Here real revenue was only between 45 and 60 per cent of that of the iron ore workers in Luxembourg. This study was followed by one of family budgets carried out by the High Authority in conjunction with national statistical bureaux and a joint committee of experts.[31] These studies of hourly wage costs, social charges and wage trends were continued. At one time the Statistical Office considered that they seemed to show that developments in the coal mines of one country sooner or later provoked analogous changes elsewhere, with the most impressive wage gains made where levels were originally the poorest.[32] It is, however, difficult to do more than hazard guesses in this matter, and the statistics of the earlier and later years are not directly comparable.

After a few years the scope of investigations began to broaden. A series of studies relating to professional, technical and managerial staff, to collective bargaining, to the modes of payment and terms of employment for non-manual workers was undertaken, and, with the collection of such information, the interest of the High Authority naturally developed from the collection of factual material to a consideration of its normative aspects. The recognition that wage improvements might come through retraining with consequential regrading of jobs, and that the old basis of allowing crude productivity to determine the wage on a piece-rate basis was becoming outmoded, led it to support new types of study to investigate the relationship between wages and productivity. These included studies of the effect of factors of remuneration such as wage structure, grading and methods of wage fixing on the productivity of the working force, whilst more detailed investigations in the iron and steel industries demonstrated the move away from physical effort towards the machine-minding process, the tendency for wage systems to move towards flat-rate payments and the effects of various methods of wage payments. Such studies were used as the basis for detailed study conferences.[33] This interest in the changing concept of wages and their relation to work done was echoed by the consultative committee. In 1956 it was asked to consider what action the High Authority might take to promote the rational linking of the structure of remuneration with the level of productivity. About 60 per cent of underground workers, or about four hundred thousand men, were getting piece rates and earning up to 20 per cent more than those on time payments.[34] Not until 1963 did the committee give its opinion on the undesirability of such linkage. At the same time it asked for new studies to be concerned with the effects of technical and social progress on payment systems.[35]

To confine studies to the field of wages would be unnecessarily restrictive. Hours worked, payments for holidays, protection against unemployment are all matters of immediate relevance to the labour situation and where some uniformity of conception was necessary as the basis for making effective comparisons. Work on legal aspects was developed by the Coal and Steel Community through the use of a working party of specialists in labour law which produced a number of documentary studies.[36]

A steady demand from mining unions during the period was for a shorter working week. The matter was first brought to the High Authority by the request of the Belgian government in 1955 that the Council should discuss the question as a possible matter in which harmonization would be desirable. This led to the initiation by the High Authority of a study of working hours and holidays in the iron and steel industry to cover regulations on working hours, the hours actually worked, overtime, holidays with pay, official paid holidays and the level of employment which, under pressure from the Assembly, was extended to all Community industries.[37] The same year work was started on a comparative survey of the provisions giving workers some security of employment and the arrangements for dismissals and the giving of notice. Finally, the High Authority cautiously began to organize meetings to which the two sides of industry were invited in order to discuss both results and national actions which would do away with the more obvious discrepancies.[38] In such ways it began to clarify the realities of existing situations and to encourage action but, as the attempt to establish the miners' charter showed, the establishment of a uniform policy for the Community area, even in a single industry, met resistance it could not overcome.

III Industrial Health and Safety

The ECSC held a special position as the initiator of much of the work of the European Communities in the field of health and safety, not only because of the particular hazards connected with the mining industry but also because of the strength of the Treaty of Paris which allowed it to develop a vigorous policy of research and education. This stemmed notably from Art. 55, which directed the High Authority to encourage research into safety through organizing contacts between research institutes, encouraging joint financing of projects, financing projects from the levy monies with Council assent and distributing research results. Arts. 46 and 47 enabled it to consult a wide range of interests and to collect all necessary information. Since it was thought that as many as one miner in ten contracted silicosis and a further three suffered from it in a suppressed form[39] the arguments for encouraging improved standards were clear.

> Quite apart from the importance of caring for the worker's physical well-being, and consequently of seeking to improve safety conditions, it is essential that efforts should be made to reduce the relatively heavy direct and indirect charges on the operating budgets resulting from industrial accidents and occupational diseases. The recruitment of workers is incidentally facilitated if the work is made less arduous and less dangerous.[40]

Its work fell into three categories. The first was the support of research projects, the second the distribution of information and the third the encouragement to governments to tighten up their laws and regulations. The Community itself had no direct right to legislate in this field although it could have issued an opinion under Art. 55. It aimed, therefore, to give a new stimulus through developing contacts between authorities and institutes already at work, through encouraging research and trying to ensure that knowledge was circulated as widely as possible. Such measures were aimed to help to prevent the duplication of research projects, enable them to dovetail into one another more readily and, by allowing all to benefit from shared experience, help to raise the standards obtaining in factory and mine. The Community was, therefore, concerned to encourage the adoption of lively and effective national policies through the revision of national legislation and the introduction of new safety techniques and preventive measures. In this respect its behaviour was confined to the traditional approach of inter-national co-operation in social matters, and consequently there could be no question of a uniform Community policy emerging, although 'on some matters it has succeeded in instituting effective and freely accepted co-ordination in respect of various projects of value to the Community as a whole'.[41]

Whilst the imposition of safety measures at the place of work is of long standing, the achievement of high standards depends upon constant attention to the impact of the changing nature of industrial processes, the turnover of personnel and the maintenance of the individual's sense of alertness and responsibility. In the daily reapplication of the principle of industrial safety the High Authority was able to find a role.

A serious mining disaster occurred at Marcinelle on 8 August 1956. On the suggestion of the High Authority, the Council decided to call an international conference on mine safety which worked from September 1956 until the following January. Representatives from the governments, employers and workers of all six countries attended and the conference ultimately passed some three hundred recommendations relating to safety in the mines which were embodied in a report submitted to the Council and the High Authority. It was clear, however, that the field of mine safety was a vast one and the conference recommendations did little more than point to the directions in which further activities would be desirable. Technical problems such as greater dust control required more research work in order to arrive at a satisfactory way of overcoming them. The training of workers in safety devices or improving rescue facilities depended on tightening up national legislation, whilst the effect of questions such as the length of the working day or the extent to which new workers might use advanced machinery raised issues of law, practice and profitability. The execution of the conference conclusions could not, therefore, be a simple matter, but on the basis of the findings the High Authority issued detailed suggestions concerning the action necessary for their implementation and at its meetings in October and December 1957 the Council passed resolutions defining the position to be adopted by governments to give effect to these propositions.[42]

A major need recognized by the conference was for an extension in the field of mine safety and this led to the recommendation that governments should create a Permanent Mines Safety Commission to keep a continuing watch on safety problems and the measures taken by national authorities to deal with them. On 9 May 1957 the Council accepted this proposition and the Commission began work the following September.

The new body consisted of twenty-four members appointed by governments.[43] Two government representatives, one employer and one worker representative came from each member, whilst the United Kingdom and the ILO also attended. Meetings were held under the chairmanship of a member of the High Authority who carried general responsibility for directing the work. The Commission acted on majority vote. A special committee, restricted to government membership, was charged with the preparation of the work and maintained links both with and between governments. Although the Commission thus had an existence independent of the ECSC, being an inter-governmental organization, it was closely related to the parent body and secretariat services were provided by the High Authority.

The Commission took over a great deal of the general work relating to the study of accidents in the mines and of the collection and dissemination of material relating to mine safety. Its main work was done through a wide range of sub-committees and study groups giving consideration to particular problems such as the technical factors contributing to accidents, for example the relation of the use of electricity underground to the fire risk of the human factors affecting safety. Reports were sent to plenary sessions of the Permanent Commission and the government committee with appropriate comments and thence, if accepted, transmitted by the delegates to governments as propositions for possible future action. During the period from 1961 to 1965 the Permanent Commission formulated sixty-one recommendations, 85 per cent of which had been adopted by all coal producing countries by 1966.[44] One of its main responsibilities was to follow the safety record in the mines. It was therefore entitled to receive information from governments concerning accidents and their safety measures and to circulate accident reports. A particular responsibility was to receive reports from member governments on the steps taken to give effect to the recommendations of the original conference and to later suggestions from the Commission.

By 31 December 1960, despite the considerable problems remaining to be disposed of and the difficulties of adapting or remodelling the safety regulations, most of the Conference's recommendations had been either incorporated into national legislation and regulations or simply applied in practice . . . only in very rare cases did one or other Government decline to make a particular change at all.[45]

In order to encourage greater awareness of safety problems and to try to ensure that relevant material was not lost in government departments but reached those working on the spot, it developed a broad educational programme for the exchange of information and experience, in addition to working with the High Authority on the establishment of a system of comparable statistics on accidents in mines and submitting ideas for research on mines safety equipment to the High Authority. Its main function was to act as a forum for exchange of information and experiences and to suggest lines of study and research to keep safety measures up-to-date.[46] Having no resources of its own, it could not itself develop research into, or experiment with, new safety devices and procedures. Finally, it submitted an annual report on its work and on the safety position in the mines to the Council of Ministers.

Union representatives on the Commission and their national organizations long wished to see an extension of its responsibilities, through interpreting safety in the widest possible sense, extending the mandate beyond the coal mines and by allowing the Commission to exercise more direct control over safety measures. The mineworkers union of West Germany was particularly anxious to see such an extension after two mining disasters in the early months of 1962. In February 299 lives were lost at Völklingen in the Saar, and the following month thirty-one miners were killed at Hessen in Westphalia. Although both the High Authority and the Permanent Commission were invited to participate in the inquiry held by the German government on the Saar disaster, these events led to a demand for the strengthening of the Mines Safety Commission. Extensions of its work were proposed by the European Parliament in a resolution of February 1962 asking governments to give the Commission further facilities and certain supervisory powers over safety arrangements in the mines and to allow it to participate in inquiries concerning mining disasters including the right to verify on the spot for itself. In 1965 it was at last agreed to enlarge the terms of reference to include industrial health in the coal mines, thus giving the Commission the right to send recommendations to governments relating to this field. It was also agreed that it had the right to concern itself with matters of industrial medicine relevant to its work, but other suggestions, including the right of direct supervisory powers over safety arrangements and the right of independent inquiry into accidents, were not accepted.[47] Since the competence of the Commission extended only to the coal mines, the High Authority itself created a steel industry safety commission with particular responsibility to arrange for the exchange of experience with a view to the better prevention of accidents. This body drew its membership from employers' and workers' organizations, was entitled to recommend necessary action and to ascertain what had been done.[48]

The High Authority embarked upon its first research programme in industrial health and safety in 1954, largely through grant aid to projects already planned by existing research institutes, but from 1957 it was increasingly able to impose its own policies. Its first programme consisted of arrangements to spend 1·2 million dollars over a four-year period in support of research projects mainly in the field of industrial health and medicine, including research into silicosis, carbon-monoxide poisoning, physiological hazards from noise and high temperature conditions, rehabilitative provisions and supply of information for industrial medical officers. By December 1955 sixty-six such schemes had been approved by means of agreements with individual research institutes to enable them to purchase equipment and pay the salaries of research workers. The Authority also agreed to organize regular discussion groups for participating research workers in order that on-going work might be constantly refreshed and seen in the context of related projects.[49] As far as achievements are concerned

> it may be recorded that Community research established the diagnostic value of the 10×10 cm X-ray film as against other formats: produced rules of spirographical practice: standardized ventilatory tests at rest; determined the incidence of pneumoconiosis in the French iron-ore mines and the degree of noxiousness of the dusts produced in the Luxembourg rolling-mills; established the functional and anatomical criteria for emphysema; developed new types of instrument for measuring atmospheric conditions; pinpointed the effects of thermal stress on kidneys; perfected devices for gauging the sound volume on particular jobs; determined the neuro-circulatory and psycho-social effects of noise, and delimited the concept of carbon-monoxide poisoning from the clinical angle.[50]

A second programme of financial assistance to research was launched in 1957 which moved into a broader field being largely concerned to improve methods of dust suppression by technical means, raise the standard of industrial safety and contribute to the rehabilitation of victims of industrial accidents and occupational diseases at a cost of three million dollars over a four-year period.

The general question of air pollution both in the coal and steel industries and by them of their surrounding areas remains one of outstanding importance and research into this problem was continuously supported by the High Authority from 1957 onwards. In that year 1·5 million dollars was allocated for this, mainly for work on air pollution within the coal industry but including studies on the reduction of dust in the transport of iron ore and in the preparation of charges for blast furnaces and on the escape of fumes on the opening-up of oxygen convectors. Grants have also been made for dust extraction illustrations.[51]

An example of research work of a very different kind was the support given by the High Authority into inquiries on the sociological and psychological factors in work accidents and the influence of work and of length of the working day on the frequency and seriousness of accidents. A summary of programmes aided by the ending of 1967 is given in Table 5.2 at the end of the section.

In order to advise it on research work and to aid the diffusion of results, the High Authority set up a scientific advisory committee in 1955. This was composed of scientific personalities currently concerned with research programmes in their own institutes and was intended to be available to give scientific and technical advice to the High Authority on its research programmes, evaluate results, advise on the selection of centres and methods and collect results in the form of reports specific to each industry. To parallel this, the High Authority also created a committee of representatives of employer and worker organizations to lay down the broad outlines of measures to be taken by the High Authority with due regard to the needs of coal mining and of the iron and steel industries and to submit any pertinent suggestions as to the type of research to be carried out. Together, these two committees produced a joint memorandum establishing the basic principles of the Authority's early policy towards research. It defined the criteria to be used in selecting the organizations best qualified to carry out the research work required, listed the problems which appeared to justify financial assistance from the High Authority and set out the methods to be employed and steps to be taken which gave promise of the best results.[52]

The High Authority evolved the broad lines of its research programme after widespread consultation which also enabled it to encourage institutes to direct part of their work so that it would fall within the general programme. The outline of its programme was published so that any centre might submit proposals, but from 1962 the Authority also tended to make direct approaches to centres where highly specialized equipment or expertise was available. It thus hoped to encourage new centres to become associated with the work and at the same time reaped the advantage of highly specialized capabilities. Although it continued to aid single projects, the Authority came to prefer to organize large-scale programmes [53] or at least to fit specific research schemes into an overall pattern so that results might become more easily comparable, enough material on parallel projects collected and the whole of a problem adequately covered. Its normal pattern, therefore, was to consult with its expert advisers and develop a definite programme which could be divided between approved research institutes. Thus its research into the causes of industrial accidents, launched in 1961, covered a wide area of study coordinated at Community level by a committee of directors aimed to ensure the use of comparable methods of work, the application of the results and their collection in the form of reports specific to each industry for ease of reference.

Since work in industrial health and safety is carried on in any case, it is hard to be precise concerning the value of the High Authority's activities. By making money available no doubt more research work was done than might otherwise have been accomplished and, through its policy programmes, it will almost certainly have influenced the direction work has taken. Certain practical results have been claimed by the High Authority. One example of this was the research on human factors affecting safety carried out in a Dutch colliery which led to changes in the operation of armoured conveyors and a 22 per cent drop in the accident rate.[54] Others included the studies sponsored into the rehabilitation problems of the handicapped and into silicosis which have preceded the increased provision of facilities for those injured at work and of preventive action. Miners' lung complaints may now be taking a less virulent form due to better medical and technical measures of prevention, including dust removal and the possibility of removing those peculiarly susceptible to other work at an early stage.[55] These were fields in which the High Authority was particularly active.

Research into such problems is only useful when it is applied. This means that knowledge must be readily available in the appropriate quarters. The encouragement of contacts amongst research workers and the despatch of research results in order to stimulate more activity needed a parallel effort to see that industrial medical officers, safety officers and operatives working with dangerous machinery or raw materials were aware of the latest findings and how best to take preventive action. The High Authority put considerable efforts into projects designed to serve these ends. Information was gathered in through the discussion of research programmes and the submission of the results of all sponsored research. The Community also established the Mining Medicine Documentation Pool which began work in 1955 to receive abstracts from the world's literature on pneumoconiosis, dust control and medical problems connected with smoke. Such knowledge was distributed through monographs and research reports directed to medical, social or industrial experts, the translation of pool literature and the provision of a bibliographical and photostat service.[56] The High Authority also became associated with the international centre for information on security and industrial medicine run by the ILO, whose bibliographical and abstracting service also became available through the Community.

In addition to supplying industrial medical officers with specialized material, the High Authority compiled and distributed comparative statistical material on industrial accidents and diseases, ran information sessions on the latest developments on industrial health and safety and established a series of working parties on practical questions relating to health protection through which it kept in contact with firms' doctors. Regular conferences and study sessions were considered an important part of its educational work, in which deliberate attempts were made to bring together different types of workers so that those researching on a problem might meet with those carrying practical responsibilities and with the workers who experienced the difficulties and hazards. In such ways the High Authority aimed to raise the level of research through greater standardization of terminology, definitions, equipment and research techniques, by means of the exchange of views on scientific matters and at the same time to provide guidance for those working in the field of industrial health and safety.

Table 5.2
Research Programme on Industrial Medicine, Health and Safety as at
31 December 1967 [57]

	Date approved	Financial aid (m.u.a.)	Years covered by programme
I Industrial Medicine			
a Physiopathology and clinical medicine			
1st programme	5.10.55	1·2	1956–9
2nd programme	7. 4.60	2·8	1960–4
3rd programme	19. 6.64	3·0	1964–9
b Traumatology and Rehabilitation			
1st programme	5.12.57	0·5	1959–62
2nd programme	19. 6.64	1·8	1964–8
3rd programme	18. 5.66	1·5	1965–9
II Industrial Physiology and Psychology			
a Human factors and safety			
1st programme	5.12.57	1·0	1960–4
2nd programme	4.11.64	1·2	1965–9
b Ergonomics			
1st programme	4.11.64	2·0	1965–9
III Industrial Health			
a Dust prevention in mines			
1st programme	5.12.57	0·9	1960–3
2nd programme	21.12.64	6·0	1965–8
b Dust prevention and suppression in iron and steel industry			
1st programme	5.12.57	0·6	1960–3
2nd programme	14. 6.67	4·0	1962–6
c Sundry projects		approx. 3·0	various
TOTAL		29·5	

IV Housing

The contribution made by the High Authority towards the solution of the housing problems of coal and steel workers represented one of its most positive features. The inadequate housing conditions of post-war Europe were particularly obvious in the regions of heavy industry struggling with the legacy of the poor building of early industrial days and war-time destruction of property. Shortage of capital for the construction of workers' housing combined with a situation in which the building industry found itself fully stretched, often unable to meet the demands made upon it for private housing and penalized by its inability to abandon craft methods of production in favour of modern mass production techniques.[58] In consequence, at the time of its introduction the

ECSC found its workers experiencing the problems of slum-living, over-crowding, family separation and very long journeys to work characteristic of a period of absolute shortage and poor material standards. A sample survey carried out on behalf of the High Authority in 1958 suggested that about 10 per cent of Community workers were then living in sub-standard accommodation requiring urgent replacement. Bad conditions were especially marked in Belgium, France and Germany. 86,000 workers had a journey of over one hour to work; 73,000 were separated from their families; over half a million were over-crowded and 118,000 workers lived without running water. Seventy per cent of dwellings had no wash basin, bath or shower. One-quarter of the accommodation was owned by the employer, a particularly common feature of the mining industry, and 40 per cent of the dwellings in use had been built before 1918, a very high proportion of them in Italy. 150,000 units were thought to be urgently needed to replace sub-standard accommodation and a further 30,000 to replace those pre-1918 dwellings not worth repairing.[59] This inquiry formed the basis of the policy objectives and building programmes drawn up by the High Authority and suggested the importance of initial con-centration on the replacement of temporary accommodation, meeting shortages and providing minimum standards of amenity.[60] Migrant workers in the Community were particularly badly housed. In 1958 22 per cent of foreign workers (excluding frontier) were living in communal accommodation for single men. The number who had acquired family homes varied from 63 per cent in Belgium to 11 per cent in Germany. Overall, the migrant worker was considerably worse off than the national worker in coal and steel (see Table 5.3).[61]

Table 5.3

Comparison of Type of Private Accommodation of National and Migrant (Excluding Frontier) Workers[62]

| | Percentage of national workers housed in | | | Percentage of foreign workers housed in | | |
| | houses in single and multi-family occupation | furnished lodgings, hostels, etc, | temporary accommoda-tion | | | |
	A	B	C	A	B	C
Germany	90·8	6·8	2·4	78·1	15·9	6·0
Belgium	97·1	2·0	0·9	76·1	16·9	7·0
France	94·5	1·2	4·3	85·6	6·6	7·8
Italy	95·5	1·2	3·3	—	—	—
Luxembourg	97·1	2·2	0·7	94·8	5·2	—
Netherlands	86·3	11·7	2·0	79·6	15·4	5·0
Community	92·4	4·9	2·7	80·8	12·0	7·2

Under these conditions the High Authority gave major priority to the question of the contribution it might make to the relief of housing shortage through financial aid to schemes designed to enlarge the housing stock available to workers in the coal and steel industries. This did not mean that it would itself build, own or manage houses, but that it would enable existing institutions to undertake a greater amount of work. National arrangements to help those unable to obtain accommodation on the open market were well-developed but diverse. Of dwellings completed in individual countries in 1969, for example, Belgium subsidized 51 per cent; Germany 37 per cent; France 77 per cent; Italy 9 per cent; Luxembourg 28 per cent and the Netherlands 85 per cent.[63] Building was normally carried out by a variety of charitable or self-help organizations, and it was mainly through control of their access to capital and borrowing terms that governments influenced the extent to which the needs of the economically weaker sections of the community were met. Control over resources, however, additionally enabled governments to influence the development of the housing sector as a whole, and public interest has by no means been confined to the sole objective of rehousing those in greatest need. Policy may be to encourage home ownership, as has been done in West Germany, as a contribution to political stability or, as in France, to compel occupants to pay more directly for their housing in order to destroy a rent restriction system which was contributing to the notorious decay of the housing stock. In consequence rent increases in France during the period were particularly heavy. Taking 1958 rents as a base index of 100, by 1969 levels had become 174 in the Netherlands, 215 in Italy, 298 in France, 196 in Germany and 148 (estimate for 1967) in Belgium.[64] The role of the High Authority was thus affected by national situations, the importance and objectives of public housing policies, the availability of real resources, the ease with which capital could be raised and the existence of institutions involved in the provision of social housing and its functioning dependent upon close co-operation with a wide range of national institutions.

Its major contribution was to supplement national schemes of low-cost housing[65] through 'programmes of financial assistance making capital available at low rates of interest to certain organizations',[66] whose form and amount varied, in order to fit in with existing methods of financing housing programmes and the pattern of banking and credit institutions.[67] Since the provision of houses was the function of low-cost housing agencies, Community loans required the unanimous consent of the Council under Art. 54 (2) relating to the financing of works and installations contributing directly and primarily to increasing production, reducing productive costs or facilitating marketing. Such assistance was mainly in the form of loans, although part of the money provided for the experimental schemes was in the form of non-repayable grants. In addition to the use of its general powers to borrow and its ability to guarantee loans raised by approved bodies, the High Authority drew upon its special reserve fund, made up of the interest received on its own investments and outstanding loans, its income from fines and the interest on the late payment of dues.[68] It was thus able to lend at low rates, often 1 per cent, and on favourable repayment conditions. Of less importance in scale was the use of monies from the readaptation account to provide loans for alternative accommodation for workers who had to transfer to other areas.[69] Having ear-marked money from its reserves, the High Authority then raised further sums on the capital markets and/or encouraged other institutions to participate in the projects. Its aid was always limited to a proportion of the total cost, never exceeding half and normally between 20 and 30 per cent, designed in part to stimulate the flow of normal capital. The schemes accepted for grant aid always took advantage of all forms of state aid and were those recognized as forming part of the national housing programme. Thus in 1964 the High Authority agreed to part-finance houses themselves part of a larger scheme to resettle from Decazeville. It lent 1·4 million French francs at 1 per cent interest for twenty years to the *Société des Habitations à Loyer Modéré* which supplemented this aid from other French agencies.[70] It was also prepared to persuade a local bank, social security fund or other capital supplier to lend money on favourable terms to a particular project, either to substitute for, or to complement, its own activities, and was particularly successful in France in encouraging the banks to lend money at reduced rates.[71] In 1959 it lent 20 million Luxembourg francs to the *Caisse d'Epargne de l'Etat* for dwellings for steel and iron ore workers in Luxembourg. Half of this sum came from the Authority's own funds and was lent for twenty-three and one-half years at 1 per cent and the remainder raised by it from the *Etablissement d'Assurance contre la Vieillesse et l'Invalidité, Luxembourg* was lent for the same period at $5\frac{1}{2}$ per cent. The *Caisse d'Epargne* in turn lent the money to the particular organizations concerned to provide the houses.[72] By taking the initiative, the High Authority was able to encourage contributions from a number of sources. As part of another readaptation to aid the *Compagnie des Ateliers et Forges de la Loire* transfer workers from Assailly to St Etienne, the High Authority provided a loan of 160 million French francs at 1 per cent interest for forty years to help finance the construction of one hundred dwellings. The city of St Etienne stood guarantor, the French government made a loan on the same terms and the *Forges de la Loire* provided the sites.[73]

At the same time, the provisions of the treaty were used to encourage experimentation with building methods and the use of materials with the object of devising new techniques designed to lower construction costs. Building methods were studied and experimental construction sponsored in order to explore the possibility of rationalizing building methods and the feasibility of the standardization of prefabricated units through 'experimental schemes encouraging building research, with a view to promoting technical developments likely to result in a reduction in building costs, and in the employment of larger quantities of steel where this is economically justified'.[74] The Authority asked the Council to agree, under Art. 55 section 2 (c), to the use of monies from the levy for an experimental building programme.[75] One million units of account were allocated for this purpose at a time when the High Authority was still feeling its way towards determining its criteria for intervention in the housing field. Rather over one thousand houses, with a minimum of 50 in each chosen area, were ultimately built under the first experimental scheme. Its basic purpose was to enable a study to be made of comparative construction costs within the Community, both between areas and between different methods of house building, with the hope of ultimately establishing conclusions concerning desirable measures of both a technical and financial nature which might lead to a reduction in building costs. A subsidiary aim was to investigate the use of steel in house building.[76] A second experimental programme was decided on in 1956 when 4 million dollars from the levy, 1 million as non-repayable aid and 3 million lent at 3 per cent for periods up to thirty-five years, were allocated for two thousand dwellings in flat blocks. It continued to experiment with the use of traditional and non-traditional materials, including steel, and to try out methods of standardization and modular co-ordination. It showed that greater industrialization in the building trade was possible, including more use of prefabrication, and reported favourably on the use of steel.[77]

Any significant reduction in housing costs is itself an important contribution to attempts to bring adequate housing facilities within reach of the whole population. However, research carried out in the experimental programmes suggested that striking differences in the average cost of house building within the Community, being relatively cheap in Germany and expensive in Luxembourg and France,[78] were not so much due to differences in the actual cost of the identical unit built in the identical way, which 'were found to be not nearly as large as had originally been assumed'.[79] Rather did they arise from the variation in the cost of productive factors and the use of techniques which did not economize on factors locally expensive and from variations in the cost of land.[80] Dwellings built were not in fact identical for there was no uniform housing unit built for workers in the Community and the variety of organizations involved in the provision of low-cost housing increased the diversity of standards in use. Customary differences in ideas about floor space, number of rooms or heating arrangements combined with variations in the availability of local materials, land prices and degree of urban development to make for very considerable variations in costs, so that the

> considerably variation in accommodation requirements and habits, the
> technical, administrative and financial arrangements prevailing in the
> individual Community countries and the diversity of the capital
> markets combined to produce major differences in the scale and effects
> of the High Authority's assistance.[81]

Whilst it is unrealistic to argue for standardization of housing construction over such a vast area, this nevertheless appears a field in which
the interchange of ideas and the use of the controlled experiment are
particularly useful as means of increasing efficiency and improving
standards.

Like any housing authority, the ECSC found itself caught in the
situation created by developing housing need. Rising standards of living
are expressed through improvements in quality and design, in amenities,
lay-out and environment, and when combined with population movements and the need to replace an old housing stock can lead to a situation
in which the satisfaction of needs recedes despite growing attempts to deal
with the problems. Thus by 1963 the High Authority found that needs
were greater than reported in the 1958 survey. A further 280,000 units
were now required since 180,000 were below standard, 40,000 needed
because of new and expanded activity and 60,000 to meet replacement
requirements and turnover of personnel.[82]

One function of the High Authority was to encourage good housing
design. In 1959 it launched a competition for architects who were required
to submit schemes for a worker's house which would be suitable for erection anywhere in the Community under public housing schemes and
adapted to modern town planning requirements.[83] Its fifth general building programme was devised to encourage a wider consideration of housing
construction, since it was partially aimed at the support of schemes paying
attention to estate lay-out, communal services and amenities rather than
being solely concerned, as hitherto, with the construction of new housing
units [84] and, of course, it retained a general interest in the design and
lay-out of all dwellings whose construction it was helping to finance.

At a time when a bigger production of coal was considered urgent, it
was important to replace outworn buildings and to build more, especially
at growth points, in order to keep or attract a sufficient labour force.
Thus labour turnover, and the heavy reliance on migrant labour, forced
the High Authority to pay some attention to the disadvantages inflicted
on the newcomer when he came to acquire housing accommodation. His
lack of knowledge and linguistic skill, his greater difficulty in raising a
mortgage, his inability to fulfil residence qualifications or other requirements of access to low-cost housing schemes as has happened if his family
stays behind all penalize him severely, and although there is some
tradition of employer-provided hostel accommodation for the single man

special measures are almost certainly required if the migrant family is to have access to housing facilities on equal terms with national residents.[85] The 1965 study of the mobility and adaptability of migrants suggested that housing provision was a crucial factor in determining whether they would settle satisfactorily, but also demonstrated the tendency for them to be less well housed than their indigenous counterparts.[86] Although all governments extended at least some of the benefits of their national legislation on subsidized housing to non-nationals,[87] often some form of positive discrimination is in practice necessary if they are to find themselves in a position truly comparable with that of long-standing inhabitants, but the High Authority's aid for the migrant was dependent upon national programmes. 'Its aid is, however, only a contribution to the whole, and given in accordance with the laws of the country concerned, and whose laws do not always allow denizen workers the same benefits as the country's own nationals'.[88]

Two other aspects of the work of the High Authority must be noted. Firstly, its housing activity brought it into close contact with agencies operating at lower than the national level of government. Since housing conditions varied from one district to another it was necessary to work out programmes in each locality. This implied the involvement of the local community to determine the number of houses to be built, site location, lay-out and design, the balance of rented accommodation and house ownership and the level of rents or repayments. Local knowledge was needed, too, to help scrutinize tenders, choose builders, advise on local housing associations, oversee building operations and ensure that the houses went to coal and steel workers.

> Right from the outset, therefore, all processes connected with the planning, building and allocation of dwellings have been fully decentralized. Loan applications were submitted to the High Authority by various national and regional bodies, while the individual countries and coal fields have national and regional committees of Government, employers' and workers' representatives.[89]

When the High Authority decided to broaden its objectives in order to encourage greater interest in estate lay-out, it again needed to establish national working groups. These included in their membership the directors of national building research establishments, representatives of local housing associations, architects, town planners, public officials, representatives from ECSC regional committees, housewives and advisers on specific questions. Similarly, local groups brought together representatives of the builders, planners, suppliers of essential services and social amenities including shops, schools and leisure facilities.[90]

In the second place, the High Authority was able to play a limited part in influencing housing policy through the selection of projects. In one sense, of course, the limitations on its actions were circumscribed by the

fact that it was not itself directly providing houses. Grant-aided institutions retained responsibility for management, rent collection and sale of
houses according to their own ideas, and, since they also required more
capital than that provided by the High Authority, schemes in which it
was interested also had to meet approval from elsewhere. Nevertheless its
views on housing policy were important. It considered workers should
have the opportunity for home ownership [91] or, if this were not possible,
that rented accommodation should be provided by bodies other than
employers: 'It intends for its part to continue encouraging whatever
arrangement may best serve to free the workers from the disadvantage of
unduly close interdependence between job and accommodation'.[92] Finally,
as previously mentioned, it tried to improve the quality, design and lay-out
of houses 'setting an example to all concerned, which will be of assistance
in the eventual working-out of a rational housing policy throughout the
Community'.[93] In mining areas rented accommodation has been very
common. *Le pourcentage de logements d'entreprises est particulièrement
élevé dans les charbonnages (près de 70% en Italie, 60% en France et
40% en Allegmagne)',*[94] and it is therefore significant that the High
Authority tried to avoid encouraging the spread of such property [95]
believing that the demand for home ownership would be one way in which
higher material standards would be expressed. About one-third of dwellings constructed with aid from the High Authority were owner-occupied.[96]

High Authority aid was given through a series of building programmes
based on an assessment of housing need in relation to the number of
workers employed.[97] By December 1970 finance had been allocated for
the construction of 113,029 units, 60 per cent for rent and 40 per cent for
ownership, whilst 106,546 houses had been built.[98] These figures suggest
that about 8 per cent of the labour force may have benefited from High
Authority aid. The first building programme was launched in 1954 and
directed towards the replacement of inadequate housing and the relief of
immediate problems. It covered the construction of 14,875 units, including 11,775 for coal miners, and included sixteen hostels for unmarried
workers in Germany. The second programme, agreed upon in 1956, aimed
to build 20,000 units, to which the High Authority agreed to contribute
15 million units of account and raise a further 15 million u.a. on the open
market, although these sums were later increased. This scheme saw the
first decision to use monies from the special reserve fund in order to keep
interest rates as low as possible. The fourth programme also covered
20,000 dwellings for which the High Authority agreed to provide 15
million u.a. from its own funds and to raise 30 million elsewhere.
Although primarily concerned with the replacement of bad housing which
the survey results had shown to be so necessary, it included aid to assist
men to move from one colliery to another as part of readaptation
schemes. It also considered, for the first time, the needs of men in iron

and steel. The fifth programme saw a steep jump in the cost to the High Authority of housing loans which reached 75 million units to offset rising building costs. In addition to grant aid in association with readaptation schemes, a special feature was the encouragement to neighbourhood planning, estate amenities and better housing standards. Out of a total of 25,000 units, 2,300 on six building sites were to be part of a special operation which would pay particular attention to the equipment of dwellings and standards of noise, privacy and design and of community amenities such as parking facilities and open spaces. The sixth scheme aimed to help housing in expanding areas, to assist resettlement and to alleviate housing shortages at a cost of 20 million units from the reserve fund with extra capital being raised on the open market if required. The seventh programme was decided upon in 1969, to run from 1970 to 1974, of which the first part was to cost 10 million units and to include a small experimental programme of house modernization.[99]

From the beginning the High Authority assumed it would have a contribution to make to social housing programmes, and the central core of its work remained the traditional function of public authorities, namely to support those who had difficulty in meeting their needs on the open market. It accepted, too, that this was a continuing responsibility since rising house prices meant that rents continued to absorb a high proportion of workers' incomes. Its schemes, however, had other objectives. The final destruction of inadequate or badly placed housing together with building in expanding areas were aims distinct from compensation for the economic weakness of the family.[100] The drive to lower construction costs, which demanded technical examination of building methods, studies on a comparative basis and experimental construction, was perhaps motivated by the desire to bring housing costs within the average pocket, supported by an interest in encouraging the use of steel. Adequate housing bore an obvious implication for an effective manpower policy, the stability of the labour force, the integration of migrants and the encouragement of workers into expanding areas of work, and its proper concern with such issues led the Authority into activity designed to encourage productivity growth in the building industry to improve construction methods, to investigate the possibilities of industrialized building, uniformity of standards and the use of prefabricated components, to ensure attention to siting and lay-out as well as housing standards. Its recognition that greater prosperity would increase the demand for better houses was a positive feature of its concern with the improvement of living standards. Its understanding that the realities of the situation demanded that serious attention should be paid to housing enabled it to exploit the treaty to undertake work of which there had been no direct mention, although it must be remembered that it was dependent upon the willingness of members that such work should be done. It established an important precedent for the larger Community to follow since few would deny the importance of adequate housing to improve living standards for the population.

A NOTE ON THE IMPORTANCE OF HIGH AUTHORITY AID

There was a steady rise in the cost of house building each year between 1960 and 1967, except in Germany in 1967. As a result, the index of the cost of house construction in 1967 was considerably above that in 1958 in each member. This was due to the rise in interest rates and site values, higher building standards and increases in the cost of materials and labour. In old established industrial areas where housing was often poor, rents were correspondingly low and new housing thus represented a very severe increase for families. With rents absorbing perhaps 30 per cent of income, many coal and steel workers required assistance yet often fell into the gap between the low income groups who received help from national schemes and those who could afford market prices.[101] The importance of subsidy is shown by Table 5.4, which is based on flat blocks, each comprising 75 square metres floor space and designed for occupation by a family with two children.

Table 5.4
Rents for Worker Accommodation Built in 1963 [102]

	Germany (D.M.)	Belgium (Bfr.)	France (Ffr.)	Italy (L.)	Luxem- bourg (Lfr.)	Netherlands (Hfl)
Unaided	2,895[a]	21,930 [b]	4,800[c]	405,000	32,000[d]	1,615[e]
State-aided	1,865[a]	12,500[b]	3,200[c]	261,000	28,000[d]	1,215[e]
State and High Authority aided	1,680[a]	12,500[b]	3,070[c]	210,000	25,500[d]	1,085[e]

[a]   includes employers loan
[b]   High Authority aid resulted in more housing not lower rents
[b]   High Authority aid resulted in more housing not lower rents
[d]   In Luxembourg the accommodation was for owner-occupation, figures are annual charges
[e]   All state subsidized housing

Table 5.4 may be helpfully compared with Table 5.5 for average annual incomes in 1962, for workers not living in company-owned housing, married with two dependent children.[103]

Table 5.5
Workers' Average Annual Incomes, 1962

	Germany (D.M.)	Belgium (Bfr.)	France (Ffr.)	Italy (L.)	Luxem- bourg (Lfr.)	Netherlands (Hfl)
Colliery worker, underground	8,780	120,328	11,205	952,319d	—	7,244
Iron and steel worker	8,643a	118,187	10,697c	1,196,484	129,076	6,703
Ore miner, underground	7,874b	—	13,946c	1,088,193	149,224	—
Colliery worker, surface	6,604	90,466	9,295	787,187d	—	5,318
Ore miner, surface	6,457	—	10,701c	923,840	120,886	—

a   North Rhine, Westphalia.
b   Lower Saxony
c   Eastern region
d   Sulcis

6 Conclusion

The Treaty of Paris did not supersede the role of the member states, employers or unions in the promotion of human welfare. The weight of responsibility still lay within the domestic field. To this activity the High Authority made a small, but definite, contribution through the help it gave to ease housing difficulties, its readaptation programmes and its aid to improve health and safety standards. Originally designed to ensure that the unemployment attributable to the introduction of the common market could be met by the existence of adequate compensatory mechanisms, the limited notion of cash benefits increasingly merged into projects designed to aid the readaptation of the older industrial regions by the involvement of the High Authority in more comprehensive plans. The executive was proud of its work here. 'We now come to ECSC's experience with what is without doubt the Treaty's most original innovation in the field of socio-economic policy, the *readaptation/redevelopment* system.'[1] The great achievement of the ECSC was to accept the need for the evolution of its protective arrangements in the light of changing economic circumstances which demanded intervention and subsidy on a scale not envisaged at the time of signature of the Treaty of Paris to deal with the general well-being of areas, to maintain income and to promote the employability of workers. By the end of 1970, 430,000 workers had received readaptation grants totalling 150 million units of account, 113,000 dwellings had been part-financed by ECSC, and research grants for industrial safety of $5\frac{1}{2}$ million units of account had been made.[2] Thus what started off as a small part of the Community system struck at least one observer twenty years later as the most significant part of the ECSC's work.[3]

Study programmes, too, proved a positive feature in that few hard comparative facts existed in the social fields of concern to the High Authority. The right to consult, to study and to publish results constituted a valuable initiative. However, such a right must be distinguished from the right to act upon the results of such studies. This remained to be exerted at national level. The High Authority was, therefore, dependent upon the willingness of other organizations to use the material made available for the purpose of prosecuting welfare ends. In practice this meant that the major beneficiaries of the existence of the ECSC's study work were the unions. The structure thus created a natural alliance between the executive and labour organizations and it is not surprising if, once the latter had overcome their initial suspicion of the new project,[4] unions began to see the ECSC as a new means towards labour gains. Together with Assembly members they began to press for the High Authority to develop its social role.[5] However, bearing in mind the belief in the importance of cost equalization, it must be recognized that the monopoly of the demand for social improvements did not lie with labour. Thus the question of the shorter working week in the steel industry was first introduced by the Belgian government in the Council of Ministers in 1955.

The dependence for action on other organizations points to an inherent weakness in the treaty structure, suggesting that a function of the High Authority was to act in an indirect manner, being supportive of the work of other social institutions rather than adopting a primary role. This is borne out by the stress placed by the High Authority upon educational programmes. These were, of course, extremely necessary during a period in which the coal and steel industries were experiencing severe challenges to their responsive capacity. The examination by the executive of the nature and implications of industrial and technological developments did not only show the difficulties they brought but also created opportunities for the High Authority to push the measures taken to deal with the problems in the direction of European integration. The necessary adjustment 'must be a steady, deliberate process based on Community measures and arrangements under common Institutions. For although the lifting of national barriers is of course a precondition for a unified European economy, it has been found to be far from enough in itself.'[6] Changes in productive techniques, including the extended use of automation, continued to affect the coal and steel industries throughout the period. Their influence on the employment situation, particularly of the elderly and the unskilled worker, provided a focus of interest for much of the High Authority's work. Some of the studies, such as those on trends in social security, the impact of technological progress or methods of payment were clearly designed to direct attention towards change, whilst the permanent exchange of information, ideas and experience which it encouraged may also have made it progressively easier for the competent national authorities to absorb a wider range of experience and to adapt to new situations. The High Authority pursued an active information and publicity programme, including the organization of seminars, the granting of scholarships, the running of conferences and the provision of films, booklets, handouts, speakers and study trips.[7] Its minimal obligation to publish the results of its grant-aided research was extended by a programme of biblio-graphical publication, whilst its policy of utilizing study groups and national research institutes itself brought more people into contact with the Community. Such arrangements served as a means both of raising the standards of competence in a particular field and of spreading knowledge about the Community itself.

Its attempts to establish a European forum for employer–worker relationships falls into a similar category. Whilst the very existence of the Community was designed to encourage fundamental changes in industry and therefore made it necessary to consider at a European level questions of how to protect workers against loss and of how to improve efficiency, these demands were interwoven with the need to develop support for the European idea.

> Thus the Community introduces into Europe both a new policy aiming to remove existing suspicions held by labour concerning employers and a fruitful collaboration to replace the forms hitherto demanded by progress. As a result, labour will be able both to give and to receive much more than has been possible up till now. The role of labour must grow with the development of the Community.[8]

Although the extent to which employers and workers became more international or more progressive in their outlook cannot be measured, one President of the High Authority thought that joint discussions helped to reveal the existence of many similar problems and suggested that concerted action might be helpful.[9] 'The development thus started is bringing far-reaching changes in the ways of thought, the modes of action and even the actual structure of the employers' and workers' organis-ations.'[10] From this point of view, the High Authority may well have had an important catalytic function encouraging the emergence of more forward-looking labour policies. It demonstrated recognition of the fact that questions of training, retraining and resettlement could no longer be left to individual firms in times of rapid technical and economic change, for fear that they would be too prone to take a narrow view, to find the cost irksome and to feel that they reaped no benefit. Another agency was therefore needed in order to take a wider view of the general welfare and to consider the relationship between re-employment policies and the welfare of a region as a whole.

Apart from its specific, fairly small-scale activities and its general educational work, it is not possible to attribute credit for an improved standard of living directly to ECSC social policy, in the sense in which the term is used in chapter 1. There was no adequate pressure to ensure the adoption of a policy of equalization and the one serious bid for it in the miners' charter came to nothing. The ability to implement such a policy would have implied that employers were no longer responsible for major policy decisions and it was, therefore, too sensititive to have any chance of success. In any case, the experience of the High Authority shows that there were two major practical difficulties in the way of the adoption of an equalization policy had this been permitted by the treaty. The first was the problem of determining the basic facts upon which any such policy would have had to build. Even in a field as much studied as social security, the High Authority was driven to admit that 'taking social security as a whole, we can hardly even determine precisely whether since the Treaty came into force the positions in the different countries have drawn closer together or the reverse'.[11] Secondly, such a policy could not have been promoted for the coal and steel industries alone. The conclusion must be that the emphasis in the treaty system was on the improvement rather than the equalization of living standards through the contribution the Community might make to economic prosperity. Since the treaty was silent about the mechanism whereby the goal was to be achieved, it must be assumed that its implication was that this aim was the responsibility, in the main, of the member governments and of the bargaining process. When it is recalled that states had also reserved their control over the free movement of labour, the totality of restrictions were such that the High Authority was necessarily driven to attempt to develop a moral authority and to win the co-operation of organizations which held effective social power.

> The High Authority, for its part, realises the special function it may be called upon to perform in the interplay of forces determining the level of living and working conditions. . . . Standing as it does in possession of the full picture, in a position to discern where a balance can or should be achieved, in process of demonstrating, by its regular study and documentation work, the extent and accuracy of its information, the High Authority is ready . . . to hold the ring, its authority accepted rather than imposed, and likely to be asserted and proved effective in negotiation, failing recourse to legal bases which the letter of the Treaty does not provide.[12]

Neither the economic changes resulting from the common market, nor the deliberate action of the High Authority seem to have led to any obvious process of 'levelling-up' for the workers in these industries. In 1957 the High Authority had noted that a

> convergence in the levels of wages in the coal mining industry was observed at one stage: this is the normal effect of the Common Market. . . . But as a result of the recent general development this tendency has been in part reversed, and the correlation between wages in the Common Market industries and wages in the other industries in the same countries has induced a bigger increase in the wage costs of the Belgian than in those of the German collieries. Instead of being closed, the gap between these costs has widened.[13]

Five years later it still believed that it was impossible to substantiate the theory that the common market would bring an automatic levelling-up of social standards.[14] If the equalization aim of the treaty is to be taken as a serious social goal, the problem would therefore seem to be one of finding more effective ways of achieving it through giving ECSC itself greater powers to act either directly or through the control it is entitled to exert over other agencies. Alternatively, one can simply accept equalization as an aspirational not a political aim. This is not to denigrate the importance of the High Authority's documentation, informational and educational work, to decry that its grant aid influenced national policies and may have done so in such a way that they began to converge in similar directions. The High Authority may well have helped to create a more favourable climate within which more definite co-ordination could be attempted. However, it does not appear that these efforts were adequate to ensure a greater degree of harmonization of social standards. Certainly no definite policy towards this end was formulated.

Any deliberate policy of redistribution would have to face the problem that those with more advanced standards would need to mark time. The High Authority avoided this issue by arguing that the way to equalization was for the conditions of the most disadvantaged to improve the most quickly within a general advance.[15] It does not seem ever to have spelt out the radical implications of this viewpoint nor to have admitted that the advance of the most favoured might well be slower than would otherwise have been the case. It did, however, realize that any European social policy would be of a broad, guideline character in view of the variations in national patterns and priorities.

> The realization of a European social policy is compatible with the recognition that both ends and means differ to some extent from one country to another. It does nevertheless presuppose that Europe has reached a reasonably similar level of development in the technical, economic and cultural fields, that there is close co-operation in European institutions and that governments have similar aims. Any collective bargaining agreements at European level, which would be a decisive step on the path of harmonization, would not be of a precise nature but rather act as a framework or as a guide. It would be more a question of a model, allowing for all the exceptions required by situations actually existing in the various countries.[16]

The prime determinant of social policy was the Treaty of Paris. Its concern with partial integration necessitated a limited view of what social policy is about by emphasizing the link with economic policy and confining the area of social policy to a concern with employment problems. The view that 'the principal components of social policy [were] wages, social security and terms of employment'[17] was the only tenable one, since the High Authority necessarily had to consider man in his role of worker. Even here, however, social policy was not rooted in the nature of the problem but in the competences derived from the treaty.

It was saved from stagnation firstly by members' recognition that Art. 56 required amendment and secondly by the powers of initiative which the High Authority possessed. The willingness to exercise them in the social field and to adapt policies according to a changing situation meant that social policy was not merely static and repetitive but was influenced by *'une interpretation positive des textes'*.[18] The levy enabled the High Authority to support research projects and to undertake a number of actions designed to aid the unemployed as well as to create new employment through investment and reconversion projects. Its ability to consult different authorities, to receive their suggestions, to make studies and to publish gave it the freedom to create committee structures through which wide contacts might be maintained.

The High Authority was, therefore, not solely a passive administrator of pre-determined responsibilities but one determinant of ECSC policy capable of changing its emphasis over a period of time. At first it concentrated its energies on housing, the free movement of labour and readaptation issues.[19] By 1966, however, it was giving special attention to problems of adult and managerial training, to the effects of mechanization and automation on the labour force, to the development of rational housing policies for a number of regions, to the reception and training of migrant workers and to the definition of principles for accident prevention in iron and steel. It launched a new programme of medical research into the treatment and rehabilitation of workers suffering from burns and stepped up its documentation work on developments within the members in the field of industrial relations and on the terms of employment.[20] It is worth recalling that neither housing nor occupational training were specifically mentioned in the Treaty of Paris although they formed a major part of the High Authority's social actions as the executive came to see the type of social need that existed. The former was one of the most interesting achievements of the Community. Its significance does not lie only in the demonstration of the capacity of an international organization to grant aid house construction but in the contribution it made to ideas concerning building methods, design and estate lay-out as well as in its ability to work with primary bodies concerned with housing provision for the less well off members of the Community. Further examples of the constructive use of the Treaty of Paris range from the broad interpretation of permitted study programmes to allow investigatory teams of employers and workers to travel to Great Britain and the United States, to the use of Art. 95 (1) to provide temporary assistance for short-time work and the amendment of Art. 56 to give a wider scope for the readaptation procedures. It cannot be said that such a wide range of activities would have sprung automatically from the treaty itself or that it would necessarily have followed from the economic changes experienced by the coal industry. Something must be allowed for the fact that the High Authority considered the social provisions of the treaty important and was generally alerted to the importance of considering the social aspects of the economic system with which it had been entrusted. Although economic pressures would have no doubt required some consideration of the manpower issue, it is not unreasonable to suggest that the work of the High Authority improved the quality of the response. It saw a role for social policy not only in the prevention of adverse social consequences of economic change but in its use in order to influence the evolution of the common market in that direction which would further improve standards of life and work.[21]

On the other hand, where principles were vague and powers uncertain, as over the harmonization issue, development was inhibited.

> But looking back over all that has happened since 1952, we cannot but see that the Community has progressed when the High Authority has been able to exercise its own direct and definite powers. This is confirmed by the results of its policy on investment and research, on cartels and concentration, on readaptation and redevelopment.[22]

There is a striking contrast between the measures used to stimulate action to deal with redundancy and the difficulties encountered over the miners' charter or the attempt to create a free labour market in the coal and steel industries. This last was left by the treaty to inter-state agreement with the result that 'the matter has been handled so gingerly that the practical effects of the measures adopted are almost negligible'.[23] It is difficult not to agree that the successes were due 'to the fact of ECSC's definite practical powers and financial independence – a principle indispensable to any future development of a true Community policy'.[24] Given this impregnable base, however, the experience of the High Authority shows that it is perfectly feasible for an international authority to play a positive role in social development provided it has good relations with states, unions and employers and can become involved in action at a local level.

The limitation of the Treaty of Paris to one economic sector demonstrated the difficulty of operating a social policy for one group of workers in isolation from the general well-being. It was impossible for social security for migrant workers to be considered on any basis other than a comprehensive one; even the issue of social security costs for employers, originally raised as a part of the problem of government subsidy to the coal industry, raised the question of employer responsibility throughout industry. Neither had the survey work undertaken by, or on behalf of, the High Authority in fields such as wage levels or terms of employment full significance except in relation to the consideration of the labour force as a whole. The extension of interest is most obviously illustrated by the positive role of the High Authority in redevelopment projects designed to improve the general economic health of an area. In the same way it can be argued that readaptation and training procedures were beneficial to the whole community in so far as they helped in the larger processes of maintaining employment, preventing pockets of un-employment and under-consumption and of aiding a smooth transition as the labour force moved from direct production into more sophisticated industries. All in all it seems that there was a positive gain for the general well-being in that the work of the High Authority helped to create a greater awareness of social issues and provided an example of practical action, and because its work could not always be strictly confined to the coal and steel industries themselves. As an economic policy affecting coal and steel could not be developed except in terms of a general energy policy, so in the social field improved conditions for one set of workers were dependent on, and influenced, advances for the labour force as a whole. It was impossible for any government to allow the social standards and benefits of coal and steel workers to rise too far above those of the rest of the working population. Thus policies of the High Authority must have been affected to some degree by the willingness of governments to see a general improvement and by their assessment of the repercussions on their respective national economies. 'The partial character of integra-tion has had at least one other negative consequence. This is linked to the unwillingness of governments to permit the development of distortions between the social situation of workers in coal and steel and that of workers generally.'[25] To some degree, the failure to develop a coherent view of the social aims of the Community may be laid at the door of the limits of responsibility given to the ECSC. 'This gap results in particular from the fact that the interpretive responsibility of the High Authority is limited to two industrial sectors.'[26] A major question which the experience of the ECSC therefore posed is whether, once the European movement had decided to advance towards the integration of whole economies, the way was open for more striking advances in social policy attributable to the existence of the European Communities.

Source Material

I *Publications Generally Consulted*

ECSC *Bulletin*
European Communities Commission *Bulletin*
European Community
Journal Officiel
Assemblée Parlementaire Européenne (afterwards Parlement Européen) *Débats*

II *Unsigned Articles from Bulletins*

ECSC 'Merger Treaty' *Bulletin* No. 56 (1965)
ECSC 'Politique de la Haute Autorité dans le domaine de la promotion des études et recherches concernant l'hygiène, la médicine, et la sécurité du travail' *Bulletin* No. 12 (1961)
European Communities Commission 'Memorandum to the ECSC Consultative Committee on the Community's work in connection with readaptation and redevelopment. 20 October 1967' *Bulletin* No. 1 (1968)

III *Assemblée Parlementaire Européenne: Documents*

'Rapport de la Commission des affaires sociales sur les problèmes de la réadaptation de la main d'oeuvre dans les industries de la Communauté' Session 1955–6, Doc. 26

IV *Parlement Européen: Documents*

'Rapport fait au nom de la Commission sociale sur le memorandum sur l'évolution de la question du statut européen du mineur' Session 1964–5, Doc. 78
'Rapport complémentaire sur le mémorandum sur l'évolution de la question du statut européen du mineur' Session 1965–6, Doc. 86

V *Press and Information Service of the European Communities*

Community Topics, Social Policy in the ECSC No. 20 *Réadaptation des travailleurs et reconversion des régions. L'action européenne en faveur des mineurs et des sidérurgistes* (undated)

VI *High Authority*

1 GENERAL
'The activities of the European Community' *General Report of the High Authority* (10 August 1952 – 12 April 1953)

2nd – 15th General Reports (superseded by Commission of the European Communities *General Reports*)

Evolution des salaires, des conditions du travail et de la sécurité sociale dans les industries de la communauté du charbon et de l'acier (annual) (continued by the Commission of the European Communities)

La Politique Sociale de la Communauté Européenne du Charbon et de L'Acier (March 1954)

La Sécurité Sociale des pays membres de la Communauté et les travailleurs migrants des pays tiers 4657/66/f

Les dispositions sociales dans les traités de la CEE et de la CECA 6487/60/f

Mémorandum sur l'évolution de la question du statut européen du mineur 10041/64

Mesures de réadaptation appliquées en République Fédérale d'Allemagne, en Belgique et en France. Bilan et Résultats 1960–5 (1966)

Policy Report (1965)

Quelques aspects des conditions du travail dans les industries de la Communauté (1956)

Ten Years of the Common Market for Coal and Steel (1963)

The ECSC: basis of a wider European Community (1967)

13 Années d'actions sociales de la Haute Autorité de la CECA Document elaboré a l'occasion du colloque syndical européen de Menton (February 1966) 8260/65/f

2 STUDIES AND DOCUMENTS SERIES

Comparison des Revenus réels des Travailleurs des Industries de la Communauté (1956)

Obstacles à la Mobilité des Travailleurs et Problèmes Sociaux de Réadaptation (1956)

Readaptation and Re-employment of Workers Report on a visit to the United States by a team of trade union representatives from the Community (1956)

3 PERIODICALS

Notes d'information sur les événements sociaux dans la Communauté (Evénements Sociaux) passim. nb:

'La Politique sociale de la Haute Autorité pendant les dix premières années du marché commun du charbon et de l'acier 1953–63' IX Année No. 5

'Les Actions sociales de la CECA pendant l'Année 1966' XII Année Special edition. Doc. 13424/67/1

The following articles from *Informations Statistiques* (distinguish from the later Statistical Offices *Informations Statistiques*):

'Taux d'equivalence de pouvoir d'achat à la consommation dans les pays de la Communauté en 1954' (July/August 1957)

'Enquête sur la situation des logements des travailleurs dans les industries de la Communauté' (March/April 1958)

'Evolution des revenus réels des travailleurs dans les mines de houille et dans la sidérurgie de la Communauté' (May/June 1958)

'Les salaires nominaux dans les charbonnages et la sidérurgie comparés a ceux versés dans les autres industries' (September 1958)

'Premiers résultats de l'enqête sur les budgets familiaux des travailleurs de la CECA. 1956/7' (October 1958)

4 SIGNED ARTICLES, STUDIES ETC. PUBLISHED OR CIRCULATED UNDER THE AUSPICES OF ECSC

M. Dupreyroux *Evolution et Tendances des systèmes de Sécurité Sociale des pays membres des Communautés Européennes et de la Grande-Bretagne* (1966)

P. Finet 'Harmonisation et Progrès' ECSC *Bulletin* (June 1961)

A. Wehrer 'Le principe supra-national dans le Traité CECA' Address to study session on the European Communities at the International University of

Comparative Law, Luxembourg (20 July 1959)
G. Boldt et al *Droit du Travail*

VII   *European Communities: Statistical Office*

'Situation des logements des travailleurs étrangers dans les industries de la CECA' *Informations Statistiques* (1960) No. 3
'Budgets familiaux des ouvriers de la CECA 1956/7' *Informations Statistiques. Série Statistiques Sociales* (1960) No. 1
'Revenus Réels CECA 1954–8' *Statistiques Sociales* (1960) No. 2
'Statistiques des Salaires 1959' *ibid.* (1960) No. 3
'Charges salariales et revenus réels 1954–9 CECA' *ibid.* (1960) No. 3
'Situation des logements des travailleurs CECA' *ibid.* (1961) No. 2
'Charges salariales et revenus réels 1954–60 CECA' *ibid.* (1962) No. 1
'Salaires CECA 1961' *ibid.* (1963) No. 2
'Salaires CECA 1962' *ibid.* (1964) No. 3
'Salaires CECA 1963' *ibid.* (1965) No. 2
'Salaires CECA 1964' *ibid.* (1966) No. 2
'Salaires CECA 1965' *ibid.* (1967) No. 4

VIII   *Joint Publication of the European Communities*

CEE, CECA and Euration *Conférénce Européenne sur la sécurité sociale* Vols. I and II (1962)

IX   *Commission of the European Communities*

General Report on the Activities of the Communities
Exposé sur l'évolution de la situation sociale dans la Communauté en . . . (annuel)
(These two documents contain information previously found in the General Reports of the High Authority)
ECSC *Financial Report 1967*
'Rapport sur la programme special de construction de la CECA' (1968)
'Tableaux Comparatifs des Régimes de Sécurité Sociale. Régime Mineur.'
'The effects of the reduction of manpower in the mining industry on mining social security systems and pension systems in particular' Social Policy Series (1972) No. 23

X   *Miscellaneous*

'Application of Art. 69 of Treaty of Paris' *Journal Officiel* No. 25 (1957)
'Constitution of the Permanent Mines Safety Commission' *Journal Officiel* No. 28 (1957)
'Extended list of occupations for the purpose of Art. 63 of the Treaty of Paris' *Journal Officiel* No. 89 (1963)
Council of Association between the UK and the European Coal and Steel Community *Comparison of the Social Security Systems operating in Great Britain and the Community Countries* (1968)

Bibliography

I Books

L'Année Politique (annuel)

W. Diebold *The Schuman Plan* New York, Praeger (1959)

E. B. Haas *The Uniting of Europe* London, Stevens (1958)

W. O. Henderson *The Genesis of the Common Market* London, Frank Cass Ltd. (1962)

U. Kitzinger *The European Common Market and Community* London, Routledge & Kegan Paul (1967)

L. Lindberg *The Political Dynamics of European Economic Integration* Stanford, Calif. Stanford University Press (1963)

L. Lister *Europe's Coal and Steel Community* New York, New York Twentieth Century Fund (1960)

R. Mayne *The Recovery of Europe* London, Weidenfeld and Nicolson (1970)

M. Palmer and J. Lambert (eds.) *European Unity* London, Allen and Unwin (1968)

P. Reuter *La Communauté Européenne du Charbon et de l'Acier* Paris, Presses Universitaires de France (1953)

J. J. Ribas *La Politique Sociale des Communautés Européennes* Paris, Dalloz and Sirey (1969)

L-E Troclet *Eléments de Droit Social Européen* Brussels, Université Libre, Institut de Sociologie (1963)

— *Legislation Sociale Internationale* Brussels, Université Libre, Institut de Sociologie (1952)

F. Roy Willis *France, Germany and the New Europe 1945–67* London, O.U.P. (1968)

II Articles

P. Gerbet 'La Genèse du Plan Schuman. Des origines à la déclaration du 9 Mai 1950' *Revue française de science politique* (July–September 1956)

R. Roux 'The position of labour under the Schuman plan' *International Labour Review* Vol. 65 (1952)

F. Vinck 'Industrial Conversion in the European Coal and Steel Community' *International Labour Review* Vol. 91 (1965)

K. Zawadzki 'The Economics of the Schuman Plan' *Oxford Economic Papers* (*New series*) V (June 1953) No. 2

See also EEC Source Material and Bibliography in Volume 2.

Notes

Chapter 1: Social Responsibility under the Treaty of Paris

1 See Bibliography for Volumes 1 (p. 112) and 2.
2 The text is in RIIA, *Documents 1949–50* p. 315.
3 The translation is from U. Kitzinger *The European Common Market and Community* (1967) p. 37.
4 The preparatory papers for the declaration were burnt the day before and the *travaux préparatoires* for the treaty were destroyed also. See P. Gerbet 'La Genèse du Plan Schuman. Des origines à la déclaration du 9 Mai 1950' *Revue française de science politique* (July–September 1956) p. 548 and S. Holt *The Common Market* (1967) p. 27. Hamish Hamilton.
5 F. Roy Willis *France, Germany and the New Europe 1945–67* (1968) p. 84.
6 Gerbet *op. cit.* p. 541.
7 The text of Monnet's letter of 3 May 1950, sent to MM. Bidault and Schuman in explanation of his memorandum which became the basis of the Schuman declaration, was published in *Le Monde* (9 May 1970).
8 Gerbet *op. cit.* p. 541.
9 E. B. Haas *The Uniting of Europe* (1958) deals in considerable detail with the differing reactions to the plan and the Community expressed by organized groups.
10 For press interpretation of the significance of the phrase concerning wage equalization, the terms upon which unions, other than Communist unions, were prepared to accept the plan and the various arguments concerning safeguards see especially: *L'Aube* (29 May 1950) (19 June 1950); *Christian Science Monitor* (29 May 1950) (3 June 1950) (11 August 1950) (19 April 1951); *Daily Telegraph* (18 May 1950); *Financial Times* (17 July 1950) (1 September 1950); *Glasgow Herald* (14 June 1950); *L'Humanité* (4 July 1950); *Manchester Guardian* (19 May 1950) (27 May 1950) (20 June 1950) (19 April 1951); *Le Monde* (28 June 1950) (5 September 1950) (13 October 1950) (23 October 1950) (19 May 1951); *New York Herald Tribune* (14 May 1950) (18 June 1950); *New York Times* (17 May 1950) (23 June 1950) (25 June 1950) (17 September 1950); *Observer* (14 January 1951); *The Times* (22 May 1950) (24 May 1950) (26 May 1950) (16 June 1950) (20 October 1950) (21 October 1950) (13 December 1951).
11 Pursuant to the treaty setting up a single Council and Commission, Brussels 8 April 1965.
12 ECSC *12th General Report* Introduction, Section II.
13 i.e. either France or Germany. The method of determining majority voting was altered by the merger treaty of 1965 to bring it into line with the Treaty of Rome so that the level of coal and steel production was no longer the critical factor.
14 ECSC *1st General Report* para. 12. It was made up of seventeen producers, seventeen workers, seventeen consumers and dealers together with four observers appointed by the Council (two producers, one worker and one other).

Members were appointed by the Council for a two-yearly period and sat as individuals not as representatives. The Council, deciding for itself which were the most representative organizations of producers and workers, called for the submission by them of acceptable names to twice the number of seats allocated from which the final selection was made. See *Journal Officiel* No. 81 (February 1961) p. 85/61 for Council decision on those organizations allowed to put up names. Sub-committees, of varying size, dealt with topics such as General Objectives, Labour Problems, Market and Price Conditions, Technical Research Projects.

15 ECSC *La Politique Sociale de la Communauté Européenne du Charbon et de l'Acier* (March 1954) p. 3.

16 e.g. a joint meeting held in November 1965 at the request of the consultative committee to discuss the social aspects of the measures introduced by the treaty.

17 J. Monnet quoted in ECSC *La Politique Sociale . . ., op. cit.* p. 4.

18 *European Community* (1966) No. 2, p. 11.

19 M. Palmer and J. Lambert (eds.) *European Unity* (1968) p. 264.

20 ECSC *La Politique Sociale . . ., op. cit.* (1954) p. 3.

21 ECSC *Readaptation and Re-employment of Workers* Studies and Documents (1956).

22 This visit took place in 1961 and was intended to develop managerial ideas on matters such as personnel and administrative patterns in business and help to break down ideas confining management to technical problems. See *European Community* (1966) No. 4, p. 13.

23 Schuman quoted in A. Wehrer *Le principe supra-national dans le Traité CECA* Address to study session on the European Communities at the International University of Comparative Law, Luxembourg (20 July 1959) p. 13.

24 Palmer and Lambert *op. cit.* p. 262.

25 P. Reuter *Organisations Européennes* Paris (1965) p. 184 *et seq.* Presses Universitaires de France.

26 Between 1954 and 1963 High Authority aid amounted to 14 per cent of the total capital expenditure in Community industries. ECSC *11th General Report* para. 402.

27 i.e. one receiving an absolute majority of votes in the Council including that of a major producer.

28 Abstracted from ECE *Economic Bulletin for Europe* Vol. II, No. 2, p. 27 and quoted in K. Zawadzki 'The Economics of the Schuman Plan' *Oxford Economic Papers* (*New Series*) V (June 1953) No. 2, p. 159.

29 Zawadzki *op. cit.* p. 165.

30 R. Roux 'The position of labour under the Schuman Plan' *International Labour Review* Vol. 65 (1952) p. 311.

31 *ibid.* esp. pp. 291–7.

32 High Authority *The ECSC: basis of a wider European Community* (Luxembourg 1967) p. 15.

33 Recommendations of the High Authority were binding in objective but not in the means of attainment.

34 The levy, although variable, was always less than 1 per cent of the value of production (56·7 million units of account in 1954–5; 29·1 million in 1957–8; 30·6 million in 1967). See ECSC *4th General Report* financial annex, para. 6; *7th General Report* financial annex, para. 1; ECSC *Financial Report 1967*. Under Art. 50 of the Paris Treaty, the High Authority could impose increases of up to 5 per cent for each quarter's delay in paying the levy; Art. 54 allowed it to fine enterprises violating the High Authority's ban on the development of unprofitable projects; Art. 59 permitted it to fine enterprises which offended its decisions concerning the imposition of quotas in times of shortages; under Art. 91 the High Authority had the right to suspend sums due to it from defaulting enterprises. In the last resort, states were bound to enforce the decisions of the High Authority on recalcitrant firms since the High Authority had no way of insisting upon payments itself (Art. 92).

35 ECSC *7th General Report* para. 156.
36 See Haas *op. cit.* pp. 357–8 and p. 387 for his comment on labour psychology towards the coal and steel market.
37 Roux *op. cit.* p. 319.
38 P. Reuter *La Communauté Européenne du Charbon et de l'Acier* (1953) esp. p. 230.
39 ECSC *5th General Report* para. 187.
40 Extracted and simplified from Commission of the European Communities *4th General Report on the Activities of the Communities* Table 28; *3rd General Report* para. 368; *7th General Report* p. 84. (Hereafter reference to reports of the combined Commission is to *1st etc. Combined Report.*)

Chapter 2: The Social Impact of the Coal Crisis

1 ECSC *1st General Report* para. 40.
2 ECSC *4th General Report* para. 97. It meant that German and Dutch producers were taxed for the help of Belgian and Italian mines.
3 The preparatory period ran from August 1952 to February 1953, the transitional period from February 1953 to 10 February 1958. The common market for steel began on 1 August 1954.
4 Up to a total of 4,075 million lire. ECSC *5th General Report* para. 185.
5 ECSC *6th General Report* Vol. 1 (April 1958) para. 14.
6 ECSC *5th General Report* (April 1956–April 1957) para. 2.
7 ECSC *3rd General Report* paras. 101, 103, 106–8.
8 ECSC *5th General Report* para. 21.
9 ECSC *7th General Report* para. 26.
10 In 1950 coal had provided 74 per cent of the power needs of the Community; by 1964 it provided only 43 per cent and by 1969 the figure was down to 26 per cent. In 1950 9·6 per cent of the Community's energy resources had been met from foreign sources, by 1969 57·8 per cent were so met. Statistical Office *Basic Statistics* (1970).
11 ECSC *8th General Report* para 50; *14th General Report* para. 113; *Basic Statistics* (1970) Table 114.
12 ECSC *12th General Report* Introduction, Section III.
13 Parlement *Débats 1961–2* (Session 8 May 1961) p. 12.
14 ECSC *8th General Report* para. 31.
15 ECSC *12th General Report* Introduction, Section v, p. 5.
16 ECSC *10th General Report* para. 543.
17 US Dept of Health and Welfare *Social Security Systems throughout the World* (1964), EEC, ECSC and Euratom *European Conference on Social Security* (1962) Vol. I, p. 475 *et seq.* (the table on p. 503 shows clearly that in no case were miners equated to the general population for invalidity and old age pensions).
18 Commission of the European Communities 'The effects of the reduction of manpower in the mining industry on mining social security systems and pension systems in particular' Social Policy Series (1972) No. 23, Annex II.
19 ECSC *15th General Report* para. 7.
20 ECSC *5th General Report* para. 7.
21 ECSC *13th General Report* pp. 87–92.
22 ECSC *14th General Report* pp. 90–5. Also Introduction, Section IV. *4th General Report* para. 267.
23 A solution to the problem of 'excess' social security costs has been found by the evolution of a formula within the treaty provisions dealing with distortion of competition on the grounds that this might arise from public charges as easily as from direct subsidy. A general definition of distortion had been developed to deal with problems of indirect taxation based upon the principle that it existed when an industry was more, or less, heavily burdened than the average for the economy to which it belonged and when there was no corresponding over/under burdening in respect of the same industry in other

countries (ECSC *6th General Report* Vol. 1, para. 12). This standard enabled governments to accept responsibility for the heavy social security burdens carried in the coal mining industry whilst preventing the aid so given becoming large enough to ensure an advantageous competitive position.

24   ECSC *15th General Report* para. 462.

25   For precise definition see *Statistiques Sociales* (1962) No. 1.

26   *Agence Europe* (9 September 1968) No. N167.

27   The rate of increase in government expenditure on social security for miners was 8·2 per cent in 1966, 11·4 per cent in 1967, 5 per cent in 1968, 9 per cent in 1969, 8·1 per cent in 1970. *1st Combined Report* Table 8; *2nd Combined Report* para. 404. European Communities Commission *Exposé sur l'évolution de la situation sociale dans la Communauté en 1970* para. 18, p. 34 (hereafter *Social Exposé*).

28   ECSC *15th General Report* Table 25, pp. 105–6.

29   Decision 1/53 of 7 February 1953. The levy yielded 10·2 million units of account in 1953 and 13·8 million units in 1955. By 1955 Belgian collieries had received 33,619 units and Italian collieries 6,000 units from all sources. ECSC *4th General Report* paras. 98, 105. By the end of 1956 a total of 50,722 units had been collected and the readjustment schemes remodelled so that aid might be concentrated on those collieries which showed neither a profit nor high working losses. These compensation payments came to an end with the transitional period, by which time they had amounted to 44·9 million units payable by the Community matched by 86·19 million from the Belgian government. Community subsidies to aid Belgian exports amounted to 5·1 million dollars. ECSC *7th General Report* Table 16.

30   6 March 1956. ECSC *4th General Report* para. 217.

31   Art. 26 (4) of the transitional convention.

32   During 1958 short-time working in some Belgian pits reached twelve or thirteen days per month. ECSC *8th General Report* para. 138 (d).

33   ECSC *7th General Report* para. 41.

34   ECSC *7th General Report* paras. 40–6.

35   ECSC *8th General Report* para. 57.

36   These are, of course, the limits on the High Authority's grants, not the total received by the workers. The original agreement ran for the period from 1 April to 31 May 1959 and up to a maximum cost of 2 million dollars (Decision 22/59). On 1 June aid was extended to 30 September 1959 and the maximum raised to 5 million dollars for aid. It was later extended for a further month but the maximum was unchanged (Decision 41/59). 'However, discussion in the Council had revealed that several Governments had the strongest objections to the employment of Community funds for the continuation of this assistance scheme.' ECSC *8th General Report* para. 59.

37   Wehrer, *op. cit.* p. 20.

38   Under Art. 26 (4) of the transitional convention.

39   ECSC *8th General Report* para. 58.

40   *ibid.* para. 142.

41   The second method lay under Art. 96 which allowed any government or the High Authority to propose an amendment for submission to the Council. On a two-thirds majority the Council had to call a governmental conference to agree on any modification to the treaty which then needed ratification by constitutional process.

42   ECSC *8th General Report* para. 144.

43   *Journal Officiel* No. 33 (16 May 1960) p. 781/60.

44   Decision 46/59. *Journal Officiel* No. 67 (31 December 1959) p. 1327/59.

45   ECSC *8th General Report* para. 59.

46   Decision 2/60. *Journal Officiel* No. 5 (4 February 1960).

47   Decision 2/61. *Journal Officiel* No. 11 (10 February 1961).

48   *1st Combined Report* Table 8, p. 182.

Chapter 3: Protection against Unemployment

1 ECSC *2nd General Report* para. 141 (author's trans.).
2 High Authority *13 Années d'actions sociales de la Haute Autorité de la CECA* Document elaboré à l'occasion du colloque syndical européen de Menton (4–10 et 11 Févier 1966) Doc. 8260/65f, p. 15 (author's trans.).
3 'La Politique sociale de la Haute Autorité pendant les dix premières années du marché commun du charbon et de l'acier 1953–63' *Evénements Sociaux* IX Année, No. 5, p. 32. Previous applications had been refused on the grounds that the common market was not responsible for the loss of work, but from 1955 the High Authority began to interpret the rules more liberally. Haas, *op. cit.* p. 92.
4 'La Politique sociale . . .' *op. cit. Evénements*, p. 32. Workers in sixty-three coal mines, fifty-three iron and steel firms and two iron ore mines had been helped Communautés Européennes, Service de Presse et d'Information *Réadaptation des travailleurs et reconversion des régions. L'action européenne en faveur des mineurs et des sidérurgistes* (undated) p. 8.
5 Under both the transitional convention and the Treaty of Paris, the state had to contribute at least half the cost of any project unless the Council, by majority, authorized otherwise. An equal share became established as normal procedure but exceptions were made; e.g. in June 1955 the Council exempted the Italian government from paying towards the cost of readaptation aid for eight thousand workers although Italy agreed to help with their re-employment in other ways.
6 200,000 French francs for the family man; 75,000 French francs for the single miner.
7 ECSC *2nd General Report* para. 144.
8 The following account is largely based on ECSC *3rd General Report* para. 176; *4th General Report* paras. 212–13.
9 ECSC *6th General Report* para. 14.
10 *Réadaptation et reconversion . . . ., op. cit.* para. 12 (author's trans.).
11 ECSC *Etude du Dévelopment Economique des Régions de Charleroi, du Centre et du Borinage* (1962).
12 ECSC *9th General Report* para. 444.
13 ECSC *10th General Report* para. 528; *12th General Report* para. 413.
14 Representatives from the United Kingdom and the United States attended on occasion.
15 Regional Economy and Policy series.
16 *Réadaptation et reconversion . . . ., op. cit.* para. 11.
17 'La Politique sociale . . ., *op. cit. Evénements* p. 48.
18 e.g. in Belgium and France it was particularly necessary to prepare industrial sites as an incentive to new industry. European Communities Commission. *Bulletin* (1968) No. 1, Supplement, p. 10.
19 ECSC *12th General Report* para. 413; *13th General Report* para. 416.
20 'La Politique sociale . . ., *op. cit. Evénements* p. 45.
21 ECSC *9th General Report* para. 442.
22 ECSC *10th General Report* para. 530.
23 Examples include studies in Germany (Salz-gitter), Belgium (Bassins du Centre, Charleroi, Borinage), France (Auvergne-Aquitaine, Montceau-les-mines, Boucau) and Italy (Piombino, Brescia, Udine).
24 ECSC *11th General Report* paras. 502–7.
25 *European Community* (1963) No. 5, p. 7.
26 ECSC *10th General Report* paras. 531, 532. Until 1965 only 33 million units of account had been allocated for redevelopment, but in 1966 alone 52 million units were put aside for the purpose. *Bulletin* (1968) No. 1, Supplement, p. 9.
27 *European Community* (1965) No. 4, p. 11.
28 *Social Exposé 1970* para. 13. Between 1961 and 1968 about 33,500 workers from coal and steel industries obtained alternative jobs created with Com-

munity aid. *2nd Combined Report* para. 345.

29 European Communities. Commission. *Bulletin* (1968) No. 1, Supplement, p. 10. In 1968 new terms were agreed upon. The interest rate became 7 per cent and the loan repayable as from the fourth year. *Bulletin* (1968) No. 8, pp. 39–40.

30 ECSC *12th General Report* para. 370.

31 *Réadaptation et reconversion . . ., op. cit.* para. 11.

32 ECSC *15th General Report* para. 509.

33 European Communities Commission *Bulletin* (1968) No. 1, Supplement, p. 10.

34 High Authority *Doc. 6895/64fr.* (26 October 1964) Table 2.

35 Some statistics illustrating readaptation aid will be found on pp. 53–4.

36 ECSC *9th General Report* para. 433. The 1967 figure is for the period from 1 February to 31 December 1967. *1st Combined Report* para. 286; *4th Combined Report* para. 132.

37 ECSC *15th General Report* para. 389.

38 The 1966 agreement with Luxembourg allowed for an eighteen month period on full pay. ECSC *15th General Report* para. 391.

39 In the Netherlands benefit was 60 per cent of the difference between the old and the new wage. In Germany, France and Luxembourg there was a ceiling on the reference wage.

40 In Germany the period was normally twelve months but eighteen months for those over forty-five. In Belgium twelve months but eighteen months for certain elderly or handicapped workers. In France twelve months but two years for Centre-Midi miners. In Luxembourg twelve months, in Italy fifteen months. In the Netherlands twelve to thirty months according to age and length of service.

41 See, e.g., ECSC *4th General Report* para. 214 for terms given to aid workers affected by the closure of some French iron and steel firms, ECSC *5th General Report* para. 239 for agreement with Italian government concerning steel workers, ECSC *8th General Report* para. 142 for agreement concerning German miners.

42 European Communities Commission *Bulletin* (1968) No. 7, p. 20.

43 ECSC *14th General Report* para. 354.

44 ECSC *15th General Report* para. 394.

45 Those unemployed the longest were over forty-five or had no usable qualifications. Workers over fifty represented about one-third of the total unemployed as a result of the fall in the number of jobs. High Authority *Mesures de réadaptation appliquées en République Fédérale d'Allemagne, en Belgique et en France. Bilan et Résultats 1960–65* (Article 56 du Traité), pp. 10–11.

46 ECSC *13th General Report* para. 410.

47 ECSC *15th General Report* para. 397.

48 National employment statistics do not always seem to have been kept, so that the experience of those receiving Community aid cannot be compared with those who did not. High Authority control was more concerned to ensure that its grants were used in accordance with the agreement than with follow-up studies, although it made some attempt to discover the fate of individual workers through the written reports it received from national authorities and from on-the-spot visits. ECSC *12th General Report* para. 407. Its contacts with national arrangements gradually became more formalized and a number of sample surveys were done on retraining provisions, ECSC *14th General Report* para. 354.

49 Of workers laid off as a result of closure measures, 75 to 80 per cent in Belgium and France and about 50 per cent in Germany had had ECSC aid by the end of 1965. *Mesures de réadaptation . . ., op. cit.* p. 10.

50 By early 1966 220,000 coal and steel workers had been retrained and given new jobs. They had some regrets and on the whole had rather less money but healthier conditions. *European Community* (1966) No. 11, p. 5.

51 ECSC *14th General Report* pp. 288–91.

52 *Doc. 8260/65f.* p. 15 (author's trans.).

53 *Débats* iv/62 No. 48 (24 November 1961) p. 122.
54 Haas *op. cit.* p. 252.
55 ECSC *10th General Report* para. 530; *13th General Report* para. 399.
56 *Doc. 8260/65fr.* p. 20.
57 *ibid.* p. 20.
58 European Communities Commission *Bulletin* (1968) No. 1, Supplement, pp. 20–1. Memorandum to the ECSC consultative committee on the Community's work in connection with readaptation and redevelopment (20 October 1967). The low cost per job in Germany was due to the fact that half the workers, until 1966, merely transferred to other pits under the same management; the high cost for chemicals in France to setting up new industries in non-industrialized areas. A total of 53·9 million units of account had been disbursed up to 4 July 1967. By 31 December 1970 reconversion loans amounted to 204 million units and loans to finance industrial investment 639 million units. European Communities Commission *Preliminary Guidelines for a Community Social Policy Programme* Sec (71) 600 Final p. 74.
59 European Communities Commission *Bulletin* (1968) No. 1, Supplement, p. 7. Note the big leap in 1965. Also *Social Exposé 1970* para. 11.
60 European Communities Commission *Bulletin* (1968) No. 1, Supplement, Table 3, p. 17. Treat as approximate only.
61 *Social Exposé 1967* Table 10, p. 298. By 31 December 1970 156 million units of account had been spent for 430,000 workers on readaptation aid. *Preliminary Guidelines . . ., op. cit.* p. 57.

Chapter 4: Manpower and Occupational Training

1 ECSC *3rd General Report* para. 171.
2 *General Report of the High Authority* (August 1952 to April 1953). Output fell from 1,590 kilos to 1,372 kilos (1951 figures excluding Italy).
3 ECSC *6th General Report* Vol. 2, para. 174.
4 The number employed in the coal industry in 1950 and 1954 (in thousands) is shown below.

	Germany	Belgium	France	Saar	Italy	Netherlands
1950	390·8	155·9	266·3	60·0	11·8	42·5
1954	433·0	149·9	219·7	58·0	9·2	47·8

See ECSC *3rd General Report* para. 171, Table 32.
5 ECSC *6th General Report* Table 47; *15th General Report* Table 45.
6 ECSC *1st General Report* para. 32; *15th General Report* para. 341.
7 ECSC *15th General Report* para. 338; *Social Exposé1970* Annexe 1, Table 8. Between 1958 and 1970 the labour force in coal fell by 60 per cent.
8 *European Community* (1964) No. 3, p. 4; ECSC *14th General Report* para. 302.
9 ECSC *12th General Report* para. 376.
10 In 1955 10 per cent of jobs were classified as clerical, technical and managerial. In 1963 14 per cent of jobs were so classified. *ibid.* para. 378.
11 70,200 coal mine apprentices had become 10,300 and steel apprentices had fallen from 10,200 to 8,400. ECSC *6th General Report* Table 48; and *Social Exposé 1970* Annexe 1, Table 8. By 1970 there were only 100 apprentices in the iron ore mines.
12 ECSC *2nd General Report* para. 155.
13 ECSC *5th General Report* p. 30, paras. 191, 228.
14 ECSC *5th General Report* para. 224.
15 ECSC *3rd General Report* paras. 173–5.
16 ECSC *4th General Report* paras. 210, 211; *Social Exposé 1970* Annexe 1, Table 13. The 1970 figures show that, out of a total of 61,600 non-nationals in coal, 17,400 came from the Community area; of 69,100 in steel, 31,200 were Community nationals and of 1,900 in iron ore, 1,300 came from the Community. Frontier workers form a special category but unfortunately are no longer distinguished in Community statistics. In 1958 there were 10,800

frontier workers in the coal and steel industry: 3,900 Germans mainly at work in the French coal mines of Lorraine; 3,300 Belgians of whom rather over half were in the French steel works and the rest in steel and the iron ore mines of Luxembourg; 3,300 Dutchmen mostly in Belgian coal mines and a smaller number in Germany. Statistical Office 'Situation des logements des travailleurs étrangers dans les industries de la CECA' *Informations Statistiques* (1960) No. 3, p. 259. Some non-nationals may have been born in the country where they were working and/or recruited into the industry when already there.

17 In 1952 foreigners accounted for 44·1 per cent of the labour force in the Belgian coal industry, in 1957 for 48·6 per cent, in 1966 for 48·2 per cent and for no less than 69 per cent by 1970. ECSC *6th General Report* para. 27; *15th General Report* Table 47; *Social Exposé 1970* Annexe 1, Table 13.

18 'Situation des logements des travailleurs étrangers . . ., *op. cit.* Table 4.

19 *Social Exposé 1968* p. 224.

20 ECSC *5th General Report* para. 273.

21 ECSC *8th General Report* para. 152.

22 ECSC *12th General Report* para. 392.

23 ECSC *7th General Report* para. 201; *14th General Report* para. 343.

24 ECSC *10th General Report* para. 502.

25 ECSC *6th General Report* Vol. 1, para. 43.

26 This programme was itself largely based on the conclusions of the conference 'Technical Progress and the Common Market' held in Brussels in 1960 under the auspices of the three Communities. For details see ECSC *10th General Report* para. 508 *et seq.*

27 ECSC *12th General Report* para. 383.

28 ECSC *2nd General Report* para. 155.

29 e.g. a Community manual of new technical processes in steel for use in the training of skilled workers designed to be published in the four Community languages. *1st Combined Report* para. 270.

30 e.g. its comparative study on the structure and organization of general and technical education in the countries of the Community. ECSC *8th General Report* para. 151. Also its series on the personnel, structure and training required in various occupations such as blast furnaces, steel works, mechanized coal faces (April 1960). See too ECSC *9th General Report* para. 419. Also sample survey of occupational retraining schemes in coal and steel. *1st Combined Report* para. 271.

31 ECSC *6th General Report* para. 213.

32 The two occupations were that of hewer (coal mines) and keeper (blast furnaces). ECSC *10th General Report* para. 504; *8th General Report* para. 151.

33 ECSC *12th General Report* para. 390; *13th General Report* para. 382.

34 *1st Combined Report* para. 273.

35 *Social Exposé 1968* para. 20.

36 Its quarterly educational service and bulletin (in collaboration with the International Centre for Information and Research in Occupational Training) is the means for this. The Centre, at Turin, was founded in 1961 by the ILO and the Council of Europe and is supported also by the Organization for Economic Co-operation and Development (OECD) and the European Communities. ECSC has participated in its work since 1962 and in 1965 decided to make regular grants to the Centre, which engages in a variety of tasks including acting as a research centre, training officers from developing countries and arranging meetings for training officers and other specialists. In 1966 the High Authority and the Turin Centre began to consider the training needs of African and Latin American nationals. See *1st Combined Report* para. 274.

37 ECSC *3rd General Report* para. 205. The coal study was published in 1966. *4th General Report* para. 232.

38 ECSC *7th General Report* para. 201.

39 ECSC *9th General Report* para. 420. The proposals covered films (including

microfilms and slides), wall charts, scale models, posters, maps, plans, drawings and sound recordings and it was hoped it would not be confined to the needs of the Community industries but cover the educational field in general.

40 Recommendation 64/412/CEE *Journal Officiel* No. 112 (14 July 1964). It included the broad definition asked for and also hoped that 'temporary import' might be interpreted generously.

41 ECSC *6th General Report* para. 214.

42 *ibid.*

43 ECSC *13th General Report* para. 373.

44 ECSC *14th General Report* para. 338.

45 ECSC *13th General Report* para. 374.

46 ECSC *13th General Report* para. 375.

47 See 'Obstacles to Labour Mobility and Social Problems of Resettlement' *International Labour Review* (1956) Vol. 76, pp. 73-4. This puts Art. 69 (1) firmly within the context of the need to soften the impact of the creation of the common market.

48 ECSC *2nd General Report* para. 147.

49 ECSC *La Politique Sociale . . ., op. cit.,* p. 11 (author's trans.).

50 Roux *op. cit.* p. 317.

51 ECSC *12th General Report* para. 431.

52 ECSC *3rd General Report* para. 183.

53 ECSC *1st General Report* para. 103.

54 ECSC *2nd General Report* para. 148.

55 *ibid.*

56 *Journal Officiel* No. 25 (12 August 1957).

57 ECSC *3rd General Report* para. 184.

58 ECSC *4th General Report* para. 219.

59 ECSC *10th General Report* para. 516.

60 *Journal Officiel* No. 89 (15 June 1963).

61 ECSC *10th General Report* para. 515.

62 ECSC *3rd General Report* para. 184.

63 ECSC *7th General Report* para. 189.

64 ECSC *14th General Report* para. 324.

65 ECSC *Obstacles à la Mobilité des Travailleurs et Problèmes Sociaux de Réadaptation* Luxembourg (1956). This was directed by the UNESCO Institute of Social Sciences, Cologne and carried out by Sozialforschungsstelle an der Institut national d'etudes démographiques, Paris; Istituto di Scienze economiche Universität Munster, Dortmund; Institut de Sociologie de l'Université de Liège; presso l'Università del Sacro Cuore, Milan; Nederlands Instituut voor praeventieve Geneeskunde, Leyden.

66 ECSC *6th General Report* para. 187 summarizes the provisions.

Chapter 5: The Improvement of Living and Working Conditions

1 Later joint committees for each industry were set up to compare conditions of work for non-manual workers. ECSC *13th General Report* para. 442.

2 ECSC *13th General Report* para. 443.

3 ECSC *3rd General Report* para. 197.

4 *Journal Officiel* No. 13 (10 June 1955) p. 783, para. 28 of the resolution on social questions.

5 For the importance attached by the High Authority to such studies see 'La Politique Sociale . . ., op. cit. Evénements* pp. 7–10.

6 High Authority *Quelques aspects des conditions du travail dans les industries de la Communauté* Luxembourg (February 1956).

7 ECSC *4th General Report* para. 223.

8 DM 2·50 per shift for piece workers, DM 1·25 for other underground workers. ECSC *5th General Report* para. 215.

9 *ibid.* para. 229.

10 Largely the responsibility of Paul Finet. ECSC *14th General Report* para. 1. The High Authority worked very closely with union representatives to formulate these proposals.

11 ECSC *13th General Report* para. 345.

12 *Journal Officiel* No. 29 (8 May 1959) p. 557.

13 ECSC *5th General Report* para. 188.

14 The story is documented in the memorandum of the Social Affairs Committee on the evolution of the question of the European Charter for Miners, presented to Parliament in November 1963 and supplementary reports thereon. Parlement Européen *Documents de Séance, 1964–5* Documents 78, 86.

15 ECSC *6th General Report* para. 255.

16 ECSC *11th General Report* para. 527.

17 Parlement Européen *Documents de Séance, 1964–5* Document 78 (19 October 1964) pp. 4–5.

18 ECSC *11th General Report* para. 534.

19 Document 78 *op. cit.* p. 5.

20 High Authority *Mémorandum sur l'evolution de la question du statut européen du mineur* Document 10041 (1964).

21 *European Community* (September 1964) p. 7.

22 ECSC *13th General Report* para. 432. See also High Authority PE Document 5999 (24 September 1964) giving the text of a letter from MM. Arendt and Van Berk to President Del Bo. This argued that since 1956 German miners had had a special bonus simply because of their status, which had had the effect of lightening the tax burden of such miners. This should not only be improved for German miners to enable them to maintain the same position they had held in 1956, but extended to all Community miners as the first step towards freeing their wages from taxation. This move would be one step towards the harmonization of living and working conditions for the miners, towards the objectives of the charter and towards the institution of a communal regime of subsidy for the miners.

23 As was freely done. ECSC *15th General Report* para. 447.

24 ECSC *3rd General Report* para. 188.

25 Hourly Wage Costs and Employers Costs for Workers in Coal Mines in 1952. ECSC *2nd General Report* Table 23. Similarly, the cost in the steel industry was significantly increased, *ibid.* Table 26. Wages and Social Charges in the Industries of the Coal and Steel Community, 1952–8. Statistical Office *Informations Statistiques* (1960) No. 1, p. 24.

26 ECSC *4th General Report* para. 221.

27 Statistical Office *Informations Statistiques* (1960) No. 1, pp. 15, 19.

28 *ibid.* p. 14.

29 *ibid.* p. 17.

30 Statistical Office 'Evolution et niveau des revenus réels des travailleurs des industries de la CECA, 1954–58' *Informations Statistiques* (1960) No. 2, esp. pp. 111, 114, 117.

31 ECSC *7th General Report* paras. 217–25 summarizes the survey. First results are in ECSC *Informations Statistiques* (October 1958). The full enquiry is found in Statistical Office 'Budgets familiaux des ouvriers de la CECA 1956/7' *Informations Statistiques. Série Statistiques Sociales* (1960) No. 1.

32 Statistical Office *Informations Statistiques* (1960) No. 1, pp. 14–15. Information is now to be found in the periodical publication *Evolution des Salaires, des Conditions du Travail et de la Securité Sociale dans les Industries de la Communauté du Charbon et de l'Acier en . . .*

33 ECSC *8th General Report* para. 157 (c); *9th General Report* para. 450.

34 ECSC *3rd General Report* paras. 190–2.

35 ECSC *12th General Report* para. 435.

36 e.g. *La Stabilité de l'Emploi dans les Pays de la CECA* (1958); *Le Contrat de Travail dans le Droit des Pays membres de la CECA* (1965).

37 ECSC *4th General Report* para. 224.

38 ECSC *5th General Report* para. 249.

39 ECSC *3rd General Report* para. 206.
40 ECSC *6th General Report* Vol. 1, para. 45.
41 ECSC *Bulletin* (1966) No. 60, p. 8.
42 ECSC *6th General Report* Vol. 2, para. 268.
43 *Journal Officiel* No. 28 (31 August 1957) p. 487. Decision of the Council of 9 July 1957 setting down the responsibilities and internal organization of the Permanent Commission for Safety in Coal Mines.
44 'Les Actions sociales de la CECA pendant l'Année 1966' *Evénements Sociaux* XII Année, para. 180.
45 ECSC *10th General Report* para. 606.
46 *1st Combined Report* para. 334.
47 Council decision of 11 March 1965 *Journal Officiel* No. 46 (22 March 1965).
48 ECSC *13th General Report* paras. 479–80.
49 ECSC *4th General Report* para. 235.
50 ECSC *8th General Report* para. 168.
51 *European Community* (1964) No. 6, p. 8.
52 ECSC *Bulletin* (1961) No. 4, pp. 45–6; *4th General Report* para. 233.
53 ECSC *15th General Report* para. 492.
54 ECSC *13th General Report* para. 481.
55 La Politique sociale . . ., *op. cit. Evénements*, p. 76.
56 ECSC *4th General Report* para. 236.
57 Simplified from *1st Combined Report* Table 18, p. 270.
58 La Politique sociale . . ., *op. cit. Evénements*, p. 62.
59 The survey resulted from a decision of the High Authority in 1957, at the request of the Assembly, to conduct an enquiry amongst coal and steel workers. The survey was carried out on its behalf by official statistical services on a standardized basis and sampled 40,000 workers out of a labour force of $1\frac{1}{2}$ million. The results were published in High Authority 'Enqûete sur la situation des logements des travailleurs de la CECA' (May/June and November 1959).
60 ECSC *8th General Report* paras. 162–3.
61 'Situation des logements des travailleurs étrangers . . ., *op. cit.* Tables 4, 5, 6.
62 *ibid.* Table 7.
63 *Social Exposé 1970* Annexe 3, Table 1.
64 *ibid.* Table 3.
65 ECSC *8th General Report* para. 163.
66 ECSC *6th General Report* para. 276.
67 *ibid.* para. 277.
68 'La Politique sociale . . ., *op. cit. Evénements,* p. 64 footnote. By 1967 total housing loans had reached 122·2 million units of account. ECSC *Financial Report for 1967* Table 12.
69 ECSC *8th General Report* para. 162.
70 ECSC *13th General Report* para. 459.
71 ECSC *7th General Report* para. 227.
72 ECSC *8th General Report* para. 159.
73 *ibid.,* para. 162 (b).
74 ECSC *6th General Report* para. 276.
75 ECSC *2nd General Report* para. 152.
76 ECSC *3rd General Report* para. 199. See also ECSC *6th General Report* para. 278.
77 ECSC *12th General Report* paras. 462, 464.
78 ECSC *6th General Report* para. 277.
79 *ibid.* para. 278.
80 ECSC *12th General Report* para. 463.
81 ECSC *6th General Report* para. 277.
82 ECSC *11th General Report* para. 547.
83 ECSC *8th General Report* para. 164.
84 'La Politique sociale . . ., *op. cit. Evénements* pp. 67–8.
85 ECSC *12th General Report* para. 459.

124   SOCIAL POLICY OF THE EUROPEAN COAL AND STEEL COMMUNITY

86   ECSC *Obstacles à la Mobilité des Travailleurs et Problèmes Sociaux de Réadaptation* Luxembourg (1956) p. 65.
87   ECSC *13th General Report* para. 350. The Belgian Royal decree of 1963 is one example. This made all Community nationals employed in the collieries eligible for the low-interest loans and non-repayable grants allowed to Belgian miners for the purpose of buying or building a dwelling provided they fulfilled certain conditions.
88   ECSC *12th General Report* para. 357.
89   ECSC *13th General Report* para. 464.
90   ECSC *11th General Report* para. 548; *13th General Report* para. 464; *14th General Report* para. 416.
91   ECSC *4th General Report* para. 228.
92   ECSC *15th General Report* para. 473.
93   ECSC *14th General Report* para. 422.
94   ECSC 'Enquête sur la situation des logements des travailleurs de la CECA' *Informations Statistiques* (May/June 1959) p. 70.
95   La Politique sociale . . ., *op. cit. Evénements,* p. 70.
96   ECSC *15th General Report* para. 473.
97   ECSC *6th General Report* Vol. 2, para. 276.
98   *Social Exposé 1970* para. 25, p. 39. The figure may be compared with the estimated need for 250,000 houses at the outset; 180,000 houses suggested in the 1958 survey or the 280,000 units referred to in 1963.
99   ECSC *5th General Report* para. 233; *10th General Report* paras. 578–81; *11th General Report* para. 548; *12th General Report* para. 467; *14th General Report* para 413; *3rd Combined Report* para. 347.
100 La Politique sociale . . ., *op. cit. Evénements,* p. 66.
101 *Social Exposé 1968* Annexe 3, Tables 3, 4; ECSC *15th General Report* para. 472; *12th General Report* para. 457; *14th General Report* para. 421.
102 ECSC *12th General Report* para. 458, Table 73.
103 *ibid.* Statistical Annex, Table 60.

Chapter 6: Conclusion

1   ECSC *Policy Report* (1967) p. 27.
2   European Communities Commission 'Preliminary Guidelines for a community social policy programme' *Bulletin* No. 4 (1971) Annex Supplement 2/71, p. 57, ECSC *Combined Report,* paras. 146, 155.
3   G. Mathieu *Le Monde* (9 May 1970).
4   La Politique sociale . . ., *op. cit. Evénements* p. 8.
5   Haas *op. cit.* p. 89.
6   ECSC *Policy Report* (1967) pp. 63–4.
7   *Journal Officiel* No. C94 (19 July 1968) Q71/69.
8   *La Politique Sociale . . ., op. cit.,* pp. 2–3 (author's trans.).
9   R. Mayer (President of the High Authority) *Address to the Common Assembly* (8 May 1956) English pamphlet edition p. 37.
10   ECSC *7th General Report* para. 271.
11   ECSC *10th General Report* para. 542.
12   R. Mayer *Address to the Common Assembly* (14 May 1957) English pamphlet edition.
13   ECSC *5th General Report* para. 7.
14   ECSC *10th General Report* para. 485.
15   *ibid.,* para. 540.
16   La Politique sociale . . ., *op. cit. Evénements* pp. 86, 89 (author's trans.).
17   ECSC *6th General Report* para. 254.
18   J. J. Ribas *La Politique Sociale des Communautés Européennes* (1969) p. 659.
19   *La Politique Sociale . . ., op. cit.,* p. 4.
20   ECSC *15th General Report* para. 334.
21   La Politique sociale . . ., *op. cit. Evénements* p. 91.

22 Signor Bo (President of the High Authority) *Address to European Parliament* (24 March 1965) English pamphlet edition pp. 7–8.

23 ECSC *8th General Report* Foreword, Section III.

24 ECSC *12th General Report* Introduction, Section III.

25 La Politique sociale . . ., *op. cit. Evénements* p. 3 (author's trans.). 4 (author's trans.).

26 *ibid.* p. 3 (author's trans.).

Index

Article 56, revision of 27, 35–6

Belgian coal industry 33–5, High Authority aid 21, 33–5, isolation from market 37, short time aid 37, stockpiling 34

Coal, demand for 25–6, effects of crisis 37–8
Court of Justice 12, 36, powers of 9

Dortmund Conference 11, 76–7

ECSC, differences of competence from EEC 1, economic objectives 12–4
Energy policy 27, 31
European Parliament 9
European unity 3–4

High Authority, acceptability to unions 7–8, capacity for initiative 105, determiner of policy 105, housing objectives 91, 92, 94, 95, 97, financing 20, importance of educative role 101, limited influence on social conditions 78, major interest in manpower 22, moral authority 103, policy on unemployment 34, powers 7, 8, 11–2, promotion of living standards 72
Housing, building methods 92, contact with work groups 95, design 94, financial aid for 91–2, 98, High Authority policy on 97, High Authority survey 90, High Authority study of costs 93, link with national policies 95–6, of migrants 90, 95, poor housing in post-war Europe 89, rising standards 94, units aided 96, use of treaty for 19

Indirect labour costs 28, 33
Industrial health and safety, application research 88, High Authority work in 82, research into 20, research programmes 85–8, strength of treaty 82

Industrial relations, European forum for 102, joint committees 72

Labour force in coal and steel, ageing of in coal 56, bonus for Ruhr miners 28, foreign workers in 58, more skills needed 56–7, size of 55

Market for coal 24–6
Menton Conference 11
Migration, free movement for skilled 65–9, housing for migrants 90, 95, principle of 19, social security for migrants 69, studies of 68–9
Miners Charter 73–8, 102
Monnet memorandum 5

Permanent Mines Safety Commission 83–5

Re-employment of redundant workers 14, 39, 42, 52
Regional redevelopment 39, conference on 42–3, co-operation over 44, financial aid for 47, High Authority policy towards 45, 48, importance recognised 41, liaison between European institutions for 47–8, reports on 44, 46, 48

Schuman Plan 4–5, economic thinking of 13–4, French attitude to 6, labour view of 16, reactions to 5–6
Social groups, contact with ECSC; consultative committee 9, housing groups 95, joint committees 72, labour organisations 11, 76–7, through information gathering 11, through research 11, 87, through studies 11, through aid to unemployed 52
Social security, burden on coal industry 28, 30, continuation of subsidies for 33, European Convention 70, for migrants 69, government aid for in relation to treaty 30–2

127